Gundog Training

Gundog Training

Paul Rawlings

Foreword by Tony Jackson

THE CROWOOD PRESS

First published in 2007 by
The Crowood Press Ltd
Ramsbury, Marlborough
Wiltshire SN8 2HR

www.crowood.com

British Library Cataloguing-in-Publication Data
A catalogue record for this book is available from the British Library.

ISBN 978 1 86126 925 6

Edited and typeset by Magenta Publishing Ltd,
Malton, North Yorkshire

Printed and bound in Singapore by Craft Print International Ltd

Contents

ORMEWOOD QUEST

23 February 1992 to 30 December 2006

In memory of a lifelong all-rounder, the only liver and white male puppy from a home-bred litter of thirteen out of black and white parents: a loyal friend, shooting companion, stud and competition dog, winner of thirty awards in field trials. Besides being an excellent worker he was a real showman who enjoyed performing in public demonstrations including the CLA Gamefair and Crufts.

Dedication

This book is dedicated to my dearest wife Lyn. Without her support for my obsession with dogs and the countryside it would never have been written.

Acknowledgements

I would like to express my thanks to the following: Tony Jackson for his inspiration and guidance; David Band for allowing me to shoot and train on his land for nearly thirty years; *Shooting Times* for having faith in my ability to write about gundog training; *Dog World* for allowing me the freedom to write about a subject I am passionate about; the numerous shooting and dog people past and present who have helped me and shared in my passion; and lastly, the trainees, human and canine, that have put their trust in me and have provided a rich source for my knowledge.

Foreword

I have long felt that in the world of gundog training, at whatever level, the premier requirement for the novice seeking to produce a dog capable of acting as a useful and productive companion in the shooting field has been an instructional guide which seeks to teach the teacher how to teach the dog!

Books on the training of gundogs almost invariably assume a degree of competence on the part of the trainer and seldom, if ever, discuss the fact that the average beginner, perhaps setting out to train his or her first gundog, simply does not know where or how to start. No one enters a school classroom in an instructional guise until they have been taught how to teach, and the same applies to gundogs and the shooting field.

Paul, as he explains in his Preface, is one of the panel of experts who, weekly, deal with readers' queries in *Shooting Times*. These are pages that I edit and, partly as a result of the continuous spate of questions and pleas for help from readers who have stumbled into the gundog training minefield and require immediate assistance and advice, and partly from the fact that Paul wrote an excellent series of articles on gundog training for *Shooting Times*, I nagged him to consider writing a book not only outlining his methods of training, but also covering the critical aspect of 'teaching the teacher'.

That he has done so in brilliant and highly readable style will be obvious to anyone who picks up this book. Paul is a thorough-going countryman, brought up in a fashion which was once familiar to many of us, though is less so today. Surrounded by dogs, ferrets and terriers, he entered with gusto into the delightful world of field sports, including coarse fishing and hunting and, surrounded as he was by his father's somewhat ill-trained gundogs, inevitably stepped out on a long and arduous path, bestrewn with pitfalls, but which was eventually to lead to field trials, competition work and instructional training. Through perseverance, skill and, most important of all, the application of the psychological approach to gundogs and their training, he has achieved pre-eminence in this field.

In my many years as a sportsman, journalist and gundog owner and amateur (*very* amateur!) trainer, I have seen and met many gundog instructors, at all levels, but the one who was, in my opinion, head and shoulders above the rest was the late Peter Moxon. It was he who, as gundog editor to *Shooting Times*, promoted a method of training which required the trainer to try to understand the dog's mind and to create an understanding that the trainer was the leader of the pack and, as such, must command the dog's love and total attention. The hideous old days of 'breaking' a dog, using the whip and a degree of force that would be quite unacceptable today, were long gone, and Peter, in my view, pioneered the humane and 'thinking' approach to the art of gundog training.

Paul Rawlings has, in my opinion, picked up the baton from Peter and is today one of the leading exponents of the 'thinking' approach to training. Never fazed by amateur would-be trainers perpetuating what may appear to be obvious, crass and basic errors, and always prepared to assist the beginner, through hard work and an intelligent approach to the training of gundogs, Paul, supported by his wife Lyn, is deservedly one of Britain's leading gundog trainers.

His experience over many years, distilled into this outstanding book, will, I am certain, ensure that it becomes a classic in its field.

Tony Jackson
Tatworth, Somerset

Preface

I believe in the importance of having a well-trained companion in the home and the shooting field. Included here is a 'pen picture' of myself that shows the knowledge I have gained through my lifelong association with field sports and working dogs.

A PEN PICTURE OF THE AUTHOR

I was born in Peterborough in 1949. My father was employed in the butchery trade and met my mother, who came from South Wales, during wartime service in the RAF.

First Introduction to Country Pursuits

Although growing up in a city, through my father's influence and his desire to make money from his sport I soon became very involved with country pursuits and the preparation of the bag for the table. I can still picture the extensive rabbit warren under an old railway carriage that had since retired from service and was then used to store the fruit boxes ready for harvest. It was there that I spent my first day involved in country sports at the tender age of five years old. I was also ferreting in the apple orchards of Wisbech, using nets and terriers. Airguns came next at six and then at the still-tender age of seven I shot my first of many Wood Pigeons, using a single barrel folding 410 shotgun made by Gallyons, which I still possess to this day.

Preparing game for the table with my father, Ted, and my sister, Jean.

At age seven with sixteen pigeons I shot over decoys with a single-barrelled 410.

Terriers

We used cross-bred working terriers as all-rounders, including all the gundog work, for filling the pot and, more importantly, for supplying my father's customers with fresh game. The strain that these leggy little dogs came from was very indistinct. The oldest, Squint, was broken coated and nearly all white, and reputedly sired by an Airedale of doubtful temperament out of a Jack Russell. Her daughter, Tinker, who was well-covered with an abundance of curly hair, was sired by a wire-haired Fox Terrier. They had a reputation in the neighbourhood for guarding the home and all tradesmen were kept at bay by the garden gate, especially the rag-and-bone man, the coalman and tinkers. The milkman seemed to be tolerated and was allowed free access, and the grocer used also to call in with no problems for weeks, but after fleeing one day with blood dripping from a tear in the seat of his trousers he never risked setting foot over the threshold of number 29 Garton End Road again.

Puppies

I have a very early and very vague recollection of spending a couple of hours snuggled up with the older terrier and her litter of very small puppies in the whelping box under the bench that my father used to butcher all his game on. The reason I was left in there so long was because the bitch decided that perhaps I was another addition to her family and her Airedale-derived temperament kept both my father and mother firmly at bay. I of course could have got out quite easily but then I was very excited at this new experience of being with the puppies, and as my mother and father by this time seemed rather agitated and annoyed I decided it was much better to stay put. Eventually the bitch was forced to go outside for a call of nature and I was quickly whisked to safety and the whelping room was immediately made toddler-proof.

Rabbits and Hedgehogs

Those terriers were quite tall on the leg, but would go to ground and dig out rabbits from the burrows, killing each one in turn before bringing them to the surface and laying them neatly in a line next to the hole then descending to locate any more that were left. They were fast enough to catch rabbits that were bolted by the ferrets and missed the nets, as could happen when two or more bolted from the same hole. They would also work like spaniels in fields of roots or along hedgerows; anything that took even the smallest amount of shot from my father's old William Evans hammer gun would be followed and retrieved, although usually lifeless when delivered, as these terriers were also adept at killing rats when necessary. Tinker also had a passion for killing hedgehogs and many a night I watched my mother pulling spines from the bitch's bleeding jaws with a pair of electrician's pliers. However, any game that fell to my father's gun was always retrieved in a fit state to be eaten and although it may have received a quick nip to stop a struggle it was not at all mangled.

Squint, my surrogate mother and guardian.

Ferrets

The ferrets were fed on sparrows and starlings, which I shot with the airgun through the window of the garden shed as they came down to feed on scraps thrown out of the family home. The terriers were excellent retrievers of these little birds and none that were wounded escaped. Strangely enough these little birds were always delivered gently and alive to my eagerly waiting hands. This was my first taste of 'gundog' work at the sharp end and I still had not reached my seventh birthday.

Squint and her daughter Tinker, the 'hedgehog killer'.

Fishing and Hunting

As a budding adolescent I became a keen coarse fisherman, winning several local junior events. I rode with the hunt in my teenage years but never got to grips with the etiquette of hunting and, much to the annoyance of the huntsman, I preferred to try to race the hounds on a little white pony that I was lent from the riding school where my sister and I used to spend every Saturday. My passion for the countryside did not sit well with the sports master at my grammar school, who believed I should have been playing hooker or scrum half for the school rugby team instead. But I had little interest in risking injury chasing a ball round a muddy pitch, especially as all the away teams seemed to consist of 6 foot Neanderthals.

The First Family Springer

My father had by this time progressed from cross-bred terriers, through pure Wirehaired Fox Terriers to a pedigree English Springer Spaniel bitch, obtained from a local farm. It had 'attitude' to say the least, in fact its temperament was more of a problem than any of the terriers. If a precious possession belonging to a family member ended up in its mouth you took your life in your hands trying to get it back. The word savage springs to mind and mercifully for the security of the family it soon suffered an unfortunate shooting accident and was never seen again. Although not having witnessed its eventual demise, personally I am not sure to this day if it really was an accident.

The First Labrador

Springers as a viable proposition were now ruled out completely by the whole family. A pedigree yellow Lab quickly arrived on the scene instead. The litter had been advertised in the local paper, so we were unaware that it had come from a puppy farm. To be fair my father, who was on the rebound from losing the Springer, may not have asked all the right questions but even so he was definitely misled at the time by the unscrupulous vendor. Although she did breed some of her own dogs, she was unable to register them since having some altercation with the Kennel Club resulting in a ban. Being somewhat of a dealer she had in fact bought the whole litter that our puppy was from just to re-sell. They were KC registered by the puppy farmers who had bred them. This little puppy was not even five weeks old when it arrived, again a fact we only discovered when the papers arrived several months later.

Father's Training Methods

Father's training methods had not changed significantly but with this more biddable pupil bursting with natural ability to retrieve and a real willingness to please the whip was unnecessary, and so thankfully was soon discarded. Candy, as she was eventually named, became a really useful all-rounder, working with the ferrets, hunting to flush game like a spaniel, and a retriever in all situations. Being an all-rounder put her in situations outside the duties of the normal Labrador's role. Her first encounter with a rat was very traumatic, as all our previous dogs had killed these little varmints without thinking, but Candy, being soft mouthed and bred to retrieve properly, ended up with the rat attached firmly on her snout and blood pouring out of the wound. My father gave her lots of encouragement to retaliate and the rat was soon bitten lifeless. This never affected her mouth when retrieving feathered game, but the odd live rabbit if it struggled after capture soon suffered the same fate! She really was an excellent dog but tragically we had to have her put down at five years old as her hips had deteriorated so badly that she was in constant severe pain. Hip screening had not come into being then.

A Dog of My Own

I always relied on the family dogs whilst I lived at home. A couple of years after marrying my wife Lyn and with the arrival of our first born, Marcus, I was able to buy my first pedigree gundog puppy, Sadi, a yellow Labrador of top class show breeding. Having previously watched my father's futile efforts to train terriers, spaniels and Labs with a biscuit in one hand and a whip in the other I decided to go it alone. I armed myself with Peter Moxon's book and set about the task of training her.

All went well in the garden, and she appeared to be obedient to my commands. She would sit and stay, was steady to a dummy, and could locate anything I hid in the garden, but then she was only six months old with adolescence just around the corner! I had taught her to beg for food, shake a paw, roll over and various other tricks that were accomplished to satisfy my own curiosity about training a dog.

I kept being drawn away from the important early chapters in Peter Moxon's book to advanced retrieving, and I made the common mistake of pushing ahead too fast, skipping the bits about obedience. I was soon scanning the book for answers to the ever-worsening problems, answers that, of course, were not there.

Over-socialization

Giving a teenager freedom soon teaches them that they can stretch parental control to the limits, and this was just the same with my adolescent Labrador who was becoming very confident outside the family pack. Exercise in the local park was going along fine until the day she realized that it was fun to play with the other dogs that joined her from time to time, when she would be oblivious to my shouts or endearing tones as I tried in vain to regain her attention. This I now know was the result of over-socialization with my father's new Labrador puppy that was about the same age. She soon found that once the constraints of the garden fence were removed and the wide-open fields beckoned there was absolutely nothing she could not get away with and my powers of control were non-existent in this new environment. Trying to teach the stop whistle and hand signals to a dog that I was unable to get near to give correction or praise is of course not the right way forward for success or harmony.

I taught Sadi various tricks but forgot obedience.

My incorrect timing of punishment also encouraged her disobedience and the messages I was giving her must have been very confusing for such a young dog. I was now in desperate need of good advice, but back in the early 1970s there were very few people that you could turn to and so my half-trained youngster was introduced prematurely to the shooting field.

This first Labrador was from a very well-known show line that is still producing winning dogs at the highest level in the ring today. However, in the 1970s the show Labs had a conformation that allowed them to do a full day's rigorous work without collapsing. My own bitch could clear five-bar gates with ease and was one of the fastest dogs I have ever owned. She began her rough-shooting career very well; she hunted through fields of sugar beet like a spaniel, well within range of my gun, and retrieved all that was shot, but of course she did this without orders and certainly was not steady to flush. This area was yet another chapter of the training book that I had skipped over completely.

Her speed at learning and physical adeptness unfortunately soon manifested into other problems. When her nose hit the scent of a cock pheasant running forward in roots she soon learned to track it by scent at the same speed as the bird could run. Having no control of this wildly developing situation, if I wanted any chance of a shot and something for dinner then I had to follow suit. Running is of course not acceptable when loaded weapons are involved and it was not long before common sense dictated that her role as a shooting dog should cease. After taking one litter from her she was returned to the breeder for use as a brood bitch, and she could well be behind many of their present day winning dogs.

Labrador Number Two

The arrival of our daughter Tanith was a good excuse for having family dog number two. I kept a yellow dog puppy out of Sadi's litter. My wife did all the early training and Max, as he was known, became the most obedient companion anyone could wish for. His only fault was that he had not inherited his mother's ability on tracking scent, or her speed. Not having that extra drive was perhaps why he was so steady and why he could only catch runners as long as he could keep them in sight. Neither would he hunt in front of me like a spaniel to flush game for my gun, but remained at all times glued to my side at heel, so now I obviously needed a spaniel to work with him.

My First Cocker

As luck would have it the shoot where I had been ferreting and beating was looked after by a single-handed gamekeeper, Jim Thompson, who was well in with some of the top spaniel field trial crowd. He worked a small liver and white spaniel in the beating line and it was just the type of spaniel I liked. It had sired some really good little workers by a first class Springer bitch belonging to one of the local tenant farmers.

On making enquiries I found that the bitch had finished her breeding career and that the pups were actually not pedigree but 'sprockers', as Jim's dog was in fact a working bred Cocker, something that was quite a rarity back then. The story goes that he had been gifted it by Jimmie Wylie as a rejected trial dog but it turned out to be an excellent worker. Jim scoured the ads in the shooting papers for me and soon located some six month old pups being advertised by a Miss Peggy Brown of 'Headland' fame, right up country in North Yorkshire. One of the dogs she had bred had recently won the Cocker Championship.

Communication was more difficult in those days and I had never travelled north of Newark before. Finally contact was made and after a lengthy conversation over a crackly telephone line (working for Post Office Telephones had some perks), I was excited to learn she had a litter of two week old pups as well as the adolescents. Although she would not commit to any sale over the telephone I sent a deposit off by post immediately, as a gesture of goodwill.

The day came and with a suitable car hired we set off on the long journey, where we were greeted at the door of Headland Cottage by Peggy dressed in a gentleman's raincoat tied up with baling twine and wearing farmers' wellington boots. The background atmosphere smelled very doggy and a huge pot of something that I later found out was obtained from the local abattoir was bubbling on the stove. I was not sure whether this was for the dogs or the tea table.

I found Peggy to be a very polite lady and her demeanour was quiet. She was obviously well educated, although the state of the cottage reflected the fact that she owned and lived with nearly thirty working Cockers. After several hours of questioning and politely drinking the strong tea that came with its own skin on top, no doubt from the natural goats' milk she was so fond of, we were eventually allowed to see the litter of eight puppies. One immediately caught my eye, a prettily marked liver and white bitch, but she seemed less forward than the others and hung back in the door of the whelping kennel.

After another hour and more 'delightful' tea and some home-made scones, finally Peggy said 'Yes, you can have one.' No, we did not then rush outside to make the selection, as Peggy insisted on telling us at length all about natural rearing and the dos and don'ts of dog ownership. Common sense now went out the window, and instead of picking one of the bolder solid coloured puppies we left with the sensitive liver and white one for the long journey home.

This poor little puppy, now christened Katy, had never seen anything in its short life other than Peggy, and Tommy, her postman. Certainly she had never been in a car before, but wrapped warmly in a towel Katy slept for hours on the long journey south.

I found out later that Peggy was very selective when it came to selling her own stock and refused to sell dogs to gamekeepers, who she said all ill-treated their poor animals, or to miners who she thought should only have terriers, whippets or pigeons and usually had families with small children. As we had small children ourselves we must have been very honoured to have been accepted as suitable and trustworthy owners for one of her beloved puppies.

Asking the Experts

This new spaniel puppy opened several doors for me and I was able to seek advice from those highly respected professionals and amateurs who were knowledgeable about this breed at that time, including John Corps, Jimmy Wylie, and Jack and Keith Chudley. I unfortunately did not listen well enough at the beginning to the sound advice freely given by my peers, and as time went on I was still struggling to find the key to my own pack leadership qualities as my sensitive little puppy was now developing a strong will of its own.

Peterborough Gundog Society

How pleased I was to learn that a new society was being formed locally to run gundog working tests and also classes to help people train their gundogs. The Peterborough Gundog Society, as it became known, flourished for many years under the leadership of Roly and June French but unfortunately was never recognized by the Kennel Club, due to some silly politics. It introduced many novices to the mysteries of gundog training and also how to run a society and its events. We all became 'experts' at dummy throwing, setting tests and stewarding and I eventually aspired to the position of committee member and then Chairman until 1983, when finally the gundog bug had taken a proper hold and field trialling was now imprinted on my brain.

Field Trials

Katy turned out to be a difficult dog to train, but I was determined and put in hours of effort. I travelled long distances to seek advice and further her education by speaking to the professionals. Although I was involved with working tests, I had never thought about field trials until one of these professionals made the comment, 'I think she has potential, you should enter her in a field trial.'

Well, that was it. I have always had a very competitive nature and so I had to go and see for myself what all the fuss was about. Cockers were not high in popularity then and so trials for them were few and far between. I contacted the secretary of the Cocker Club, George Tickner, and was heartily encouraged to join. I was immediately invited to go and watch their novice field trial that was being held the following month at How Caple in Herefordshire. A packing crate from work was soon modified into a portable travelling kennel to house the dogs in the back of the Hillman Hunter estate, the kids were packed off to granny's and Lyn and I set off with food, flasks and sleeping bags!

Most of the people who ran Cockers in those days had plenty of money, but the HQ Hotel was way out of the reach of a humble Post

Office Telephones technician so the luxury of the back of the car it was. It was an absolutely foul night, blowing a gale, and the torrential rain clattered down on the roof. But the anticipation of watching some of the top handlers in action made all that seem so insignificant at the time. How wrong we were! The whole trial took place in thick woodland, full of briar, so that apart from fleeting glimpses we never saw anything. However, we got to meet all sorts of interesting people with a common interest and everyone, without any exception, seemed really pleased to meet us and Katy, who had been allowed to come along for the day (this policy has changed in recent years).

The First Entry

So with no real knowledge of what went on I was persuaded by the Cocker Club elite to run Katy in the first Cocker Trials of the next season in October 1977 at Hensol, Lady Henderson and the late Admiral Sir Nigel's fantastic Scottish estate. Yes, another night of luxury in the back of the car!

Katy's hunting enthusiasm and dishonest nature never let us finish a trial. But thinking back, my own eagerness to show her off in the shooting field at every opportunity, where she excelled as a rough-shooting dog, and also taking her in the beating line too soon perhaps caused that. My next Cocker puppy I made so obedient and steady that it hunted at a snail's pace and I was embarrassingly put out of a trial because it was not doing the job required of a competition spaniel.

Dress Code

It is amazing the things that go through your mind when you are struggling to succeed – magic whistles, lucky ties, and so on. I had noticed on these early visits to the trials that there was a certain dress code that all the successful pros seemed to adopt, and a pair of plus twos and a ghillie's hat seemed the minimum requirements to achiėve success. My measurements carefully made, I sent off the order to Hebden Cord, who had been recommended as a supplier of shooting clothes by many of the keepers on the local estates. The breeks fitted me perfectly, but unfortunately I now had another problem as my socks were all too short. I soon acquired some shooting stockings, which were a bit on the large side, and after walking an hour or two through wet cover they would slowly stretch and wrinkle. Nora Batty was the nickname I was given by one of the other beaters (Peter Blatch) on the local shoot, who thought it was hilarious to use it whenever possible.

Success at Last

After this rather shaky introduction to field trials, I eventually won my first certificate of merit in 1979, with a home-bred but diminutive black daughter of Katy, Ormewood Penny. In peak fitness she weighed only 18lbs but her small size did not matter and she went on to win over thirty field trial awards, including winning the Yorkshire Gundog Society Open Stake under judges Keith Erlandson and Mike Cottam, and a diploma of merit in the Cocker Championship held in 1981 at Vaynor Park in North Wales, under judges Jack Davey and Danny McKenzie.

Further successes quickly followed and I made up FTCh Glenfernate Meg of Ormewood and took fourth place with her in the Cocker Championship at Bala in 1984. I then ventured into Any Variety trials, winning with several English Springer Spaniels, including Rytex Rawlin of Ormewood, Ormewood Quest and Toonarmy Trojan of Ormewood, who I qualified for the 2002 AV Spaniel Championship by winning the Cambridgeshire Field Trial Society's Open Stake under judges John Holloway and Peter Asbury.

For a time my whole aim in breeding and training my own Ormewood gundogs was driven by this fanatical urge to compete in field trials. However, I am a great believer in using my dogs fully for work in the shooting field and not just keeping them for field trial competition. I still remember, and am very grateful for, all the help and advice, much of which was freely given, when I began training and working dogs in the shooting field. I have since tutored many aspiring trainers on a one-to-one basis to help them get the best from their own dogs not only as working dogs but also as well-trained and obedient family companions.

LIFE AFTER BRITISH TELECOM

I took early retirement from BT in 1996 after thirty years' service. I now live and work as a professional gundog trainer, instructor, breeder and writer at Ormewood Kennels at Whittlesey in the Fenland district of Cambridgeshire. My wife Lyn, who besides many years supporting my interests was also Field Trial Section Secretary for the Cocker Spaniel Club until 2002, runs her own boarding kennels and cattery at the same address.

I get a great deal of pleasure in breeding and training my own puppies – Cockers, Springers and of course Labradors as well. I then get enormous satisfaction not only when one of them does well in field trial competition, but most importantly when they turn into useful shooting companions. Some stock has been exported to Europe, the USA, South Africa and Sweden. I currently own ten gundogs and have a yellow Labrador and two field trial winning English Springer Spaniels standing at stud.

When I first left BT I wondered what on earth I would do with all my free time, now it is the opposite and free time really is at a premium. Besides running my own business I do voluntary work connected with promoting dogs and shooting to enable others to have the opportunity I was given to take part in the sport.

My Contribution

When I first wrote this section of the book it looked rather like a very lengthy CV. What follows is a reduced version that only reflects a proportion of the boards, clubs and societies with which I am proud to be involved. All these organizations work towards the promotion of high standards of dog care and training

Life after BT.

A dog training and responsible ownership demonstration for the children and parents at Ashbeach School, Ramsey St Mary's.

in field sports, and are vital to the continuation of the sport and the well-being of our dogs.

I am a Kennel Club Member and sit on the Kennel Club General Committee, the Field Trial Sub-Committee and a number of working parties including the Kennel Club Accredited Instructors' Board. This scheme was launched at Crufts in 2001 and now has many accredited instructors and other members enrolled who are working towards accreditation. I am very proud to have gained my own KCAI accreditation in the spring of 2006.

I am Chairman of the Working Certificate Working Party that was responsible for developing this prestigious new Kennel Club Certificate for all working gundog owners to work to. This working party also monitors the Show Gundog Working Certificate, which is used to prove that dogs that have been successful in the show ring also retain some natural working ability.

I am an 'A' Panel Spaniel Judge, having officiated at trials in all parts of Britain, and in Ireland and Sweden, and more recently I have judged retrievers in the UK. I was delighted to be invited to judge the KC Cocker Spaniel Championship at Conholt in 2007.

I am currently Chairman of The Spaniel Club, which is responsible for organizing the annual English Springer Spaniel Championship on behalf of The Kennel Club.

When not involved with these groups I somehow find time to write regular columns for *Dog World* and *Shooting Times*. This latter work gave me an introduction to Tony Jackson, who encouraged me to write this book.

Through all these involvements I am fully committed to helping others obtain the best from their dogs.

CONCLUSION

The majority of my dog training knowledge has been accumulated through direct involvement and personal research. I am recognized by the KCAI Accreditation, which is the only nationally recognized scheme for instructors in dog training and behaviour. My methods have been proven to work but I am ever-conscious that other people's methods may achieve the same results without always having regard for the welfare of the dog. Throughout this book I will guide you through the complete course of gundog training whilst bearing in mind that my methods for early rearing, formal training, steadiness to game and so on will also produce a well-behaved family companion that may never ever go shooting.

CHAPTER ONE

Choosing the Right Dog

The factors to consider before deciding which breed to choose, including the various roles a dog may be asked to perform. The different gundog subgroups and recognized cross-breeds. Locating a breeder, registration and KC/BVA health care schemes.

The Countess of Leicester with Swazi and Sutu, family companions and working English Springer Spaniels.

FACTORS TO CONSIDER ON BREED CHOICE

When I first thought about owning a gundog my choice of breed was not based on actual experience, but on what I fancied would suit me at that time. I was a rough-shooter first and foremost, so I needed a dog that would hunt to flush game, retrieve everything I shot, sit in a pigeon hide, join me on outings with the ferrets and, most importantly, also be a family pet and companion. How I ended up with a pure show bred yellow Labrador bitch was really by accident, caused by peer pressure from my father who had a complete aversion to spaniels, but then had never seen a good Labrador either. They say a little knowledge is a dangerous thing, and I soon found that to be true. My limited knowledge, at that time, of the different breeds was mainly gained through reading all the wrong books instead of seeking expert advice. However, as a pet and a family dog this yellow Labrador bitch was excellent.

Retrievers sitting quietly by their handlers waiting for the drive to finish.

Type of Work

Wildfowling, driven shooting at the peg, in the beating line, ferreting, walking up grouse, pheasant, partridge – the list of uses to which a dog might be put is long and varied. Many shooting people do not specialize; they need an all-round gundog that can serve them in some, many or all of these different roles.

Listen to the advice and experience of others, but really the only way to form an honest personal opinion about the different breeds is by watching them in action in the shooting field and, of course, by talking to owners who keep and work them in the way that you intend to. Watching the top dogs in action at the International Gundog League Retriever Championship can be an awesome experience but remember you first have to put game up for the guns to shoot before the retriever comes into its own to put it in the bag. Spaniels are brilliant for this hunting function and, if properly trained, can sit at a peg or in the hide. Long-distance retrieving is not their forte but they are very resilient in thick, thorny cover, so are excellent at sweeping through behind the guns on a driven day.

One of the hunt, point and retrieve (HPR) breeds, which can point and hold sparsely spread wild game while the gun gets in position to take the shot, could be the choice of the lone rough-shooter who has acres of ground on which to work a wide-ranging dog. They are more specialized and need more time, training and live game to fully develop all their skills. If you are fortunate to have access to a grouse moor, or acres of partridge-holding stubbles, and if retrieving is not an essential requirement, a pointer or setter quartering a

Top retriever FTCh Drakeshead Deana and handler David Latham in action at the IGL Retriever Championship at Holkham.

beat up to 400 yards wide will save your legs while you enjoy one of the oldest forms of pure gundog work.

I personally would not recommend one of the hunting breeds if you only shoot driven game. However, for the less formal shoot, where your dog would be required to work as a beater on alternate drives, or where most of the birds shot will fall in dense woodland, a well-trained spaniel or HPR can be an ideal choice. It is not impossible to train any type of gundog solely for work at the peg of the driven gun, but it can take a much longer time to achieve any sort of satisfactory end result with a hunting breed. Better to have a Labrador or other type of retriever puppy, where years of selective breeding have produced the inherent qualities to assist success.

The modern strains of spaniel in particular have evolved to hunt forcefully through all types of tough cover in search of game. It is not easy to settle them motionless at a peg for lengthy periods, and it will be very frustrating for a 'hunting machine' to completely switch off while his master drops birds all around him. This breed of dog is more likely to fidget, make a noise or become unsteady than a retriever in this situation, especially if the training is not absolutely complete.

The Family Environment

If the dog is also to become part of the family home then make sure the breed you select will suit the environment in which you live and blend in with the family pack that it is joining. It may seem obvious that large, active dogs are not suitable to the confines of a flat in the city, but then consider that these dogs

An English Springer Spaniel retrieving over a fence with typical enthusiasm.

are sometimes kept all their life in a small kennel and run. In both cases as long as the dog has regular mental and physical stimulation it can be perfectly happy. However, a bored dog is an unhappy dog and it could soon develop bad or anti-social behaviour.

Normal Function of the Pedigree Breeds

Gundogs are split into four different subgroups, each of which has been bred to fulfil different roles in the shooting field: retriever; spaniel; pointer and setter; and hunt, point and retrieve.

Retrievers

The retriever's usual function in the shooting field is to walk or stay quietly and steadily by the handler's side until required to search for, and tenderly retrieve, shot game from locations both on land and in or over water.

Spaniels

Their usual function in the shooting field is to quarter ground in front of the handler, within gunshot range, to locate any game hiding in the cover and flush it into the open for the gun to shoot. They should subsequently be able to retrieve tenderly any game shot, if required, from all types of cover, land or water, or over obstacles.

Pointers and Setters

Their usual function is to quarter ground with a wide-ranging pattern across the wind to locate game using air scent, then point and hold it until such time as their handler is

An English Setter being cast off to hunt for partridge on the vast arable fields of East Anglia.

within shooting range, when they are allowed to flush on command. They should remain steady after the flush and are not normally required to retrieve.

Breeds which Hunt, Point and Retrieve

The usual function of a HPR breed in the shooting field is as a rough-shooting dog, often where game is sparse, when they are required to quarter the ground, locate and point game and subsequently, when their handler is within range, flush it for the gun to shoot. If required, they must be able to retrieve tenderly any game shot from all types of cover, land or water, or over obstacles.

There are also three other fairly recent imports – the Kooikerhondje, the Small Munsterlander and the Spanish Water Dog – that as yet have not been fitted into one of these subgroups, even though they are on the imported breed register. As yet, only a little is known of their function in the shooting field.

Competition

If you intend to enter field trials or gundog working tests then you will probably want a breed that is fully competitive at the highest level. The Labrador is the first choice, from the retriever subgroup, of the field trial enthusiast. It is without doubt also the most popular breed of dog in the UK, with over 45,000 now registered with the Kennel Club (KC) each year. Of course, the majority of those registered at the KC are not working dogs but fulfil the needs of family ownership as well as competing in the breed ring. The best spaniel for competition must be the English Springer, the modern descendant from the Norfolk Spaniel. However, a good Cocker is also a joy to own

A German Longhaired Pointer pointing game.

and both the English Springer and the Cocker have their own dedicated field trials in which to compete.

Trainability

Another factor when making a choice is your own experience and ability to handle and train a dog. If you are relatively inexperienced then picking one of the more popular breeds will usually help, because they are as a rule the easier dogs to train. The more difficult breeds are always going to be the choice of only the most dedicated enthusiast, until such time that careful selective breeding or the use of an outcross may perhaps produce a more biddable example, and subsequently the popularity of the breed will increase. I personally experienced this happening with the working Cockers three or four decades ago and it is also now becoming evident with Clumber Spaniels.

My final advice would be to give the decision much thought and decide wisely, as whatever choice you make is a serious commitment. If you make the right choice then hopefully the dog will still be with you after fifteen years or so of fulfilling all your needs and enjoying a happy working/family life.

THE BREEDS

As has been said, pedigree gundogs registered at the Kennel Club are split into four different subgroups. For the purpose of field trial competitions these are as follows:

- retrievers and Irish Water Spaniels;
- sporting spaniels other than Irish Water Spaniels;
- breeds that hunt, point and retrieve;
- pointers and setters.

The Chesapeake Bay Retriever excels at retrieving from water.

One of the UK's oldest native breeds, the Curly Coated Retriever.

A friendly Flat Coated Retriever, with water dripping from its coat after a retrieve from the lake.

These four subgroups each contain a huge variety of breeds, which I have listed below alphabetically, not in order of popularity.

Retrievers

Chesapeake Bay
The Chesapeake Bay Retriever is favoured by wildfowlers who need a substantial dog with inexhaustible energy and strength. It has a harsh, thick, oily coat that can withstand the coldest of water. This is an active breed that needs plenty of exercise.

Curly Coated
The tallest of the retriever breeds, the Curly Coated Retriever has a distinctive black or liver coat of tight curls lying close to the skin. It is one of the oldest native breeds, and although it is rarely seen at work in the shooting field nowadays it nevertheless has an enthusiastic following in the breed ring.

Flat Coated
This breed is well worth considering for the home or for work. I have trained several over the years and they all had a delightful, friendly disposition coupled with excellent noses; hence the breed's game-finding ability is without question. It also makes a good family companion, the coat is easy to keep clean and it fits into kennel life well.

Golden
The Golden Retriever is a very popular and versatile breed that is at home in all walks of life. However, there is a huge difference in ability, conformation and colour between strains bred for the show ring and those bred solely for work. The working strain can be

Sally Eley's working Golden Retriever, Rory.

as lithe and agile as a working Labrador, although some appear to have a more laid-back demeanour when at rest.

Labrador

By far the most popular breed of dog, in historical terms the Labrador is a relatively new introduction. It arrived in the UK in the late 1800s and has only been recognized by the KC for just over 100 years. It is the first choice of retriever for the majority of shooting folk due, no doubt, to its versatility. Like the Golden, there are distinct working and show strains. Do not expect Labradors to be as naturally placid as they are sometimes described; believe me, the placid ones have usually been very well schooled.

Lagotto Romagnolo

The Lagotto Romagnolo, which has a thick, curly coat, was recently added to the retriever subgroup by the KC due to its reputation for retrieving from water. It has also reportedly been used as a truffle-hunting dog on the continent. I know of one that has recently been trained as a gundog and is used for picking up on shoots in the south of England.

Nova Scotia Duck Tolling

Originally from Canada, this breed was brought to the UK in 1988. It has been nicknamed the 'swamp collie' by some of the other breed supporters due to its reputed way of working, whereby it swims with its white-tipped tail waving in the air to attract wildfowl within range of the guns, and subsequently retrieves any that are shot.

Mrs Cecilia Neill's Lagotto Romagnolo, which is used for picking up on shoots in the south of England.

Nova Scotia Duck Tolling Retrievers.

Spaniels

American Cocker

This breed was reputedly developed in the USA from imported English Cocker stock. These same bloodlines are also behind our own native Cockers. However, around the 1930s there seemed to be a dramatic change in type in the USA and the result is a dog that, due to its profuse coat, would not be able to work (although the odd one does occasionally work, but only after a severe haircut). As long as you like grooming they can make good family pets, but I would not recommend one for working.

Clumber

Of French origin, this is the heaviest of all spaniels. They were bred to replace beaters on driven shoots and have recently begun to regain popularity as rough-shooting companions. Two distinct types are now being developed – working Clumbers, which are much lighter and more agile, and show specimens, which tend to be heavier.

Cocker

With the largest number of registrations each year in this subgroup, the Cocker holds top place in the popularity stakes and is an excellent choice for family or work. Once again, choosing from the correct breeding lines for your purpose is essential. However, although the divergence between show and work types happened many decades ago, I still occasionally see puppies from mixed stock and pure show stock that would do a useful job of work but lack that extra drive to compete successfully in field trials.

English Springer

Unlike the Cocker, the majority of English

Chris Page's Clumber Spaniels, Hazel and George.

The author with his Ormewood working Cockers.

Springer Spaniels that are registered are from working stock, and the breed remains the top choice of working spaniel for the shooting field. It is a definite all-rounder that, with the correct training, can function as a tireless hunting machine or, conversely, sit calmly in the hide or at the peg and so fulfil the requirements of a beater or a retriever. It also makes a good but energetic family dog, and as a rule is easy to train.

Field

This is a vulnerable breed, which has survived to the edge of extinction twice. A few dedicated supporters of the breed have kept it going, and I have seen many that still retain good natural hunting ability.

Irish Water

The Irish Water Spaniel is classified as a retriever for entry in field trial competition, but as a spaniel for the show ring. This is an ancient breed, which comes in a dark liver colour and is covered in dense, tight ringlets apart from the muzzle and tail, which are smooth. They certainly do not hunt cover with the drive of the other spaniel breeds, but they are very well suited to the retrieving role.

Sussex

This is another breed that nearly disappeared, but I have seen several of these golden-liver coloured dogs at work. They are not fast, working at a thorough but steady pace with body and head low to the ground, albeit with great enthusiasm when scent is encountered. They are more at home in the beating line than as an all-rounder. They reputedly give tongue when working on fresh scent, but I have never witnessed this.

The Irish Water Spaniel.

Welsh Springer

The distinctive, rich red and white markings make Welsh Springers easy to distinguish from the other breeds of spaniel. The show and working types have not, in this breed, split significantly. The Welsh Springer makes a good family companion, and I have seen several good workers beating and picking up. It is certainly harder to train than its English cousin, and a good puppy is more difficult to acquire.

Lizzie, the Welsh Springer Spaniel who never made it as a gundog but is a lovely family pet.

Hunt, Point and Retrieve Breeds

Bracco Italiano

Powerful and strong in appearance, one can see that the Bracco Italiano has a substantial amount of hound blood in its ancestry. I have not seen one working in the field.

Brittany

One of the smallest HPRs, its square and cobby appearance gives it a very distinct, clipped style of movement when hunting. The Brittany has lots of drive and good retrieving ability. I have trained several excellent examples for shooting and falconry, and have seen others compete well in field trials in the company of other HPR breeds.

One of the smallest HPRs, the Brittany.

German Longhaired Pointer

Since it was re-introduced to the UK in the 1990s this breed has established itself as a force to be reckoned with in field trial competition, and of course as a very useful rough-shooter's dog. It is the largest of the three German pointers, with a very aristocratic appearance and traditionally undocked tail.

German Shorthaired Pointer

The German Shorthaired Pointer was the first breed of this subgroup to be imported, just after World War II. It has since established itself as the most popular choice of HPR for the shooting person. It is versatile and can function in all roles in the shooting field, but is most at home on the rough-shoot where their wide-ranging hunting ability allows them to locate and hold any game for their handler. Several dual champions have been made up – in other words, dogs that have been made up to a champion in the show ring, and have also won their title at field trials.

German Wirehaired Pointer

In its native country this is by far the most popular of the three. It has a thick, harsh outer coat that affords good protection from inclement weather and thick, thorny cover. I have seen some excellent ones competing in trials.

Hungarian Vizla

The Hungarian Vizla has a smooth, dense coat that is almost red in colour. Each HPR breed has characteristics that are unique to its breed; this breed can have the speed of a German Shorthaired Pointer, but I have witnessed others that were slower and tended to

Martin Taylor's German Shorthaired Pointer, Trudy.

Alyson Ellwood's Hungarian Vizla retrieving at Raby Castle.

An Italian Spinone relaxing with its owner at the CLA Game Fair.

drop their nose onto ground scent if allowed. This may have been a problem with training, however.

Hungarian Wirehaired Vizla
Classified as a separate breed, the Hungarian Wirehaired Vizla tends to have a heavier bone structure than the shorthaired Vizla, but still has all the same working qualities.

Italian Spinone
A pale-coloured, solidly built dog with a tough, thick coat. The ones I have seen at work seemed to be very sedate in their movement, certainly not having the speed and drive of the more well-known breeds.

Korthals Griffon
Similar at first glance to a German Wirehaired Pointer, it was refined as a breed in the Netherlands. It is an established breed on the continent, but as it has only recently been imported to the UK little is known here about its working ability.

Large Munsterlander
This is an unmistakable breed; it is black and white, with a full tail. I am told that it is derived from the same stock as the German Longhaired Pointer, the only distinct difference being the colour. It certainly has not been as successful as its brown cousin in the shooting and competition field.

Slovakian Rough Haired Pointer
This breed originated from Czechoslovakia in the post-war period, and is a cross of three breeds – the Czeskey Fousek, the Weimaraner and the German Wirehaired Pointer. It was bred during an experimental programme in the 1950s that aimed to produce a fairly close-hunting dog whose forte was to track and locate shot game. It was recognized by the Federation Cynologique Internationale (FCI) in 1982 and was subsequently imported into the UK in 1997. Although I have seen several at game fairs, as yet I have not witnessed one at work.

Gil Simpson competes at shows and trains Weimaraners for work in the field.

Weimaraner
This has become a very popular breed, particularly as a companion or pet, or as a fashion statement because of its distinctive silver-grey colouration, which appeals to those wishing to be seen with something different. I have seen some excellent workers in the hands of experienced trainers and I have trained a couple personally. They are probably better living in the house as they do not generally settle well when isolated in a kennel. Although most are smooth coated, there is a longhaired variety that also looks very attractive.

Pointer and Setters

Pointer
Although we now regard the Pointer as a truly English breed, it probably originated three centuries ago in Spain. Unlike all the other dogs in this subgroup, it has a hard, short, fine coat covering a very muscular body. The rigid pose it strikes when pointing game is unmistakable and has provided a subject for many sporting artists and photographers. This breed can still produce dual champions.

English Setter
Two distinct types have evolved – those seen in the show ring, which are much bigger, with a heavier frame and flowing coat; and those to be found working, which are very lithe and agile, with an attractive, flowing motion as they glide over the ground.

Gordon Setter
This distinctive breed, with its familiar black and tan markings, can still produce a dual champion. Most breeds of gundog are so split between show and work type that this is unachievable.

Irish Red and White Setter
This breed has recently become popular in the show world since its re-introduction to the UK, probably because of its striking red and

Colin Organ with Mr Pruden's Pointer Fernglen Fez and Miss A. Brown with Irish Setter Lusca Finn, waiting with other handlers to work their dogs on partridge.

white colouring. It is slightly heavier in build than its all-red cousin. Although not as common in the shooting field, some enthusiasts of the breed are endeavouring to rectify this, and one dog recently qualified to run in the Pointer and Setter Champion Stake.

Irish Setter
This is one of the oldest breeds, and has always been a favourite in all circumstances. Again, like the English Setter, separate strains have evolved for show or work. The breed is described as racy and that is particularly true of the field trial strains, which move with great speed over the moors seeking grouse.

Other Breeds not yet Classified into a Subgroup

Kooikerhondje
A small, red and white, medium-coated dog originally used for attracting wildfowl into the nets of a duck decoy, the Kooikerhondje originates from the Netherlands. It is similar to the decoy dogs that were historically used in East Anglia to attract fowl into the nets of the large Fen decoys, though the decoy dogs were more fox-like and were solid red. I do not know of any that work as gundogs.

Small Munsterlander
From the same region of Germany as the Large Munsterlander, it has a brown and white colouration and was originally used by falconers. It varies considerably in size, and although 35lbs (16kg) is described as normal there are too few in the UK yet to have set a standard. The first litter was born here in December 2003.

Spanish Water Dog
The Spanish Water Dog is similar to the

The Spanish Water Dogs of Joanne Milner and Sarah Gray that work in the beating line on a Lincolnshire shoot.

Lagotto in appearance, and also has a curly coat. Its appearance does not immediately enable you to compare it with any of the other dogs in any of the subgroups. At the present time three are worked regularly in the beating line on a shoot in Lincolnshire. Their work is to flush game during the drive, and at the end of each drive they will also pick up shot birds for the guns. They do not point staunchly like a Brittany, but will indicate game by scent and hesitate before flushing.

Cross-breeds

Whilst unregistered cross-breeds can make very useful pets, companion and working dogs, be aware that they cannot be registered at the Kennel Club, and therefore cannot take part in any gundog competitions. If bred from, the progeny are not necessarily going to retain the attributes of the breeds originally used and even the same cross may not produce the same type of dog again.

The list of cross-breeds is endless, due to all the different permutations that have been tried. Crossing a show strain to a working strain in the same breed could almost be considered in this category for those breeds where the separation between the two is so great. However, I will deal here with some of those cross-breeds with which I have had direct personal experience.

Spanador

Two or more variations are possible, the more common being a 'springador' (an English Springer Spaniel cross Labrador) and, less commonly, the 'cockador' (a Cocker cross Labrador). I have never trained the latter, but living in the Fens I have seen and trained quite a number of the former. I have never seen one that looked remotely like a Springer, however. They were all solid black in colour, some sported a white mark or blaze on the chest and had a little more feathering on the full tail. Every one could hunt with fantastic drive and this, coupled with the large size, makes them ideal for walking-up birds in the huge fields of sugar beet that are so common in my area. Depending on the parentage they are as a rule very trainable, as you may expect when joining two of the best breeds together.

Sprocker

This is an English Springer cross Cocker. I suspect this cross has been done many times over the years for various reasons, from cheating in trials to improving hunting qualities. Even in the present day it is sometimes difficult to distinguish between some of the smaller Springers and the larger Cockers of the black and white or liver and white colourations. The Sprocker is a useful spaniel and has all the same attributes that you would expect of its parent breeds.

Golden Retriever Cross Labrador

My son has one of these as a guide dog, which is excellent, but really it looks all Labrador and has a short coat. I have seen several in the shooting field and they all tended to favour the appearance of the Labrador. One was a very pale yellow dog that was used regularly in the beating line on a local shoot. It quartered quite freely up to a hundred yards in front of the line, it would locate game by scent, then came rigidly on point before being told to flush by its handler. I am sure that if allowed it could have won any HPR trial with ease due to this and its retrieving ability.

Collie Cross

The Border Collie has been used to add intelligence to many different types of dog and, although I have no proof that it has been used in gundogs, I have heard plenty of the old-timers talk about it being used.

I was running a little Cocker at the Yorkshire Open in a dale near Sledmere some years ago. As we worked along a narrow strip of cover at the top of the valley, I was told to stop my dog to allow a shepherd to bring some sheep through the field trial line. As the flock passed I glanced across and to my amazement the dog that was pushing them along was not in appearance a collie but a liver and white English Springer, yet its actions were akin to a proper sheepdog. I have seen many gundog cross Border Collies come into our boarding kennels, and many are indistinguishable from the gundog breed that they are from. The Border Collie genes seem to have little impact on the physical make-up of the progeny.

Labradoodle

This is a Labrador cross Standard Poodle. It is another gimmick, started because of a funny name or, more seriously, to try to produce a dog which is attractive and does not moult like a Labrador, making it more suitable for people with allergies or asthma. Considering they are mongrels, the price of these novelties is phenomenal – up to £1,000. I believe there are now strains that are three generations away from the first crosses but I am not sure whether a specific type has been established. I have never seen one at work, but the Poodle was first a working dog and is believed to be in the ancestry of several of the gundog breeds sporting a curly coat.

LOCATING A SUITABLE PUPPY

How you find your puppy will depend on whether you have decided to follow convention and buy a pedigree KC-registered puppy, or to take a chance to save money on one of the many unregistered puppies available. My advice would be to buy a KC-registered pedigree, as you will have far more safeguards in place to ensure the puppy is from tested, healthy, sound stock, and all KC-registered puppies come with six weeks' free insurance.

Health Schemes

Most breeders of the larger breeds, such as the retrievers, will have had their breeding stock tested through the KC/British Veterinary Association (BVA) health schemes which will help to identify any potential hereditary problems such as hip dysplasia or eye diseases such as progressive retinal atrophy, glaucoma and many others. Before I put you off dog ownership completely, let me reassure you that these schemes have now been effective for some time and, through responsible breeders being able to identify infected stock and remove them from their breeding programmes, the incidence of any of these problems now being very low.

Locating a Breeder

The Kennel Club website (www.the-kennel-club.org.uk) is the best place to start looking for a breeder. Its puppy sales register lists all the current litters of the breeds that you are interested in, which have recently been born and subsequently registered with them. Good advice can also be gained on all aspects of responsible dog ownership from this same source.

You can always go it alone and search the classified adverts in the press. However, just because the advert in the local paper or one of the reputable shooting magazines has puppies of your chosen breed for sale, it does not mean that they are exactly what you require. Sex, colour, age, show or work, qualifications of the parents, health-screening issues and of course the price will all influence the sale. Just because the breeder is asking a premium price does not mean they are better than some advertised a couple of hundred pounds cheaper.

Registration Documents

This is a minefield for the unsuspecting new dog owner. To avoid disappointment make sure that you act with caution until you are certain that the breeder's claims for their stock are correct. Ask all the right questions and insist on an answer. If they say the parents are hip scored then ask to see the KC/BVA certificate which they will have received after their bitch was x-rayed and put through the KC/BVA scheme, unless the puppies' registration forms have already been returned to the breeder from the KC (as these forms include all the details of the parents' health screening and the scores will be printed on them).

The registration forms and free insurance documents should be ready for you to collect when the puppies are eight weeks old and ready to go; it takes just a few days for the registration process, from sending off the completed form to receiving the documents back from the KC. Until you have seen those papers you cannot be sure that the puppy will, or indeed can, be registered even if you have seen its pedigree (which will probably have been produced in house by the breeder).

Unregistered Pedigree Puppies

Beware of getting misled – there are many pedigree gundogs born each year that for one reason or another are outside of the KC registration system and, whilst they may give a lifetime of good service, you will not have the same safeguards or opportunities that are available to the owners of KC-registered pedigree dogs.

Do not be influenced by the appealing sight of a little puppy which seems desperate for a new home. If you want a fully registered pedigree puppy, which will enable you to become involved in so many organized activities later on if the training goes well, do not settle for second best now.

CONCLUSION

Your dog will be with you for many years to come, so make sure that you choose wisely. Pick a breed to suit your lifestyle or shooting requirements and research the breed well before locating a reputable breeder. Ask as many questions as you need to before committing yourself to a particular purchase. Buy from health-tested stock and have your puppy checked by a vet.

However, just because your puppy is a gundog breed do not expect it to grow automatically into a trained one. That part of the equation is going to rely on your own efforts regarding its education.

Read on and prepare yourself for an enjoyable future!

CHAPTER TWO

How a Dog Learns

Understanding a dog's learning process and how it differs from ours. Behavioural terms and how they relate to dogs' instincts and patterns of thought. 'Operant conditioning', which is the basis of all modern dog training.

INTRODUCTION

Dog training has gone through an enormous transition over the last fifty years. 'Dog-breaking', or training dogs with 'a big stick', have been replaced with a more positive psychological approach to canine learning by the majority of modern trainers. My own proven methods have evolved over my lifetime, but I never stop being amazed by how there are always new skills to learn that can be used to solve difficult training problems effectively. My own knowledge of the current behavioural terms makes understanding research and the application of associated new training/conditioning methods much easier; in this chapter I hope to explain these terms for those who are just starting out on this most enjoyable pastime.

You may ask why it is necessary to use the jargon associated with canine behaviour; it is a question that is not that easy to answer without an understanding of the meaning of the individual terms themselves. So please persevere and study this chapter to the full, and hopefully my explanations will clarify a subject that at first glance seems complex and perhaps more than a little confusing. This chapter will also be useful for you to refer back to when one of these terms is used in the rest of the book, or indeed when talking to other dog trainers in the future.

Dogs do not have the same cognitive thought processes as Homo sapiens. They do not have the power of reason and will communicate in different ways to us. If you as their trainer get it wrong then it is impossible to explain to your dog after the mistake has been made. Therefore a deeper understanding of the dog's learning process will benefit you in the future as a trainer.

As you read the following please remember that a 'reward' to a dog is something that the dog wants, and this may often be in conflict with what the trainer thinks is a 'reward'.

CONDITIONING

Definitely not anything to do with hairdressing or grooming, conditioning is a term associated with the science of animal behaviour and is also the basic concept of all dog training. It has two distinct forms, classical and operant.

Classical Conditioning

The discovery of classical conditioning is attributed to a Russian scientist, Ivan Pavlov, who was studying dogs' digestion during the early twentieth century. By accident he observed that his laboratory dogs would salivate before food was given, and he thought that the sound of the door opening in advance of the food being given was perhaps the cue to this salivation. Over a period of time, by ringing a bell before feeding the dogs, Pavlov found that the dogs would then salivate at the sound of the bell even without food being presented. Therefore the salivation had now become a conditioned reflex.

Now the bell, before being used for the experiment, had no obvious association with food, which means it was a neutral stimulus. By associating its sound each time with the pleasure of food it then become a conditioned stimulus, which produced the reflex action of salivation without food being present. A dog will, of course, naturally begin to salivate when it tastes food, but that is an unconditioned reflex – the food is the unconditioned stimulus and the salivation is the unconditioned response.

No one could make the reflex behaviour of salivation happen by command, but by using the food as a stimulus the natural reaction is brought about. The food is repeatedly associated with the neutral stimulus (the sound of the bell) until eventually that sound becomes a conditioned stimulus. This conditioned stimulus, when heard by the dog, subsequently causes the conditioned response of salivation.

Classical conditioning affects reflex actions; these of course are not all as simple as salivation, and mostly they are associated with survival instincts – salivation aids digestion, blinking protects the eye, a loud noise causes fear reflexes, pain makes a dog run away or fight. Many of these may be accidentally induced by exposure to environmental influences – thunder, lightning and gunfire causing a fear reflex, or thorns, thistles and nettles causing a pain reflex.

Operant Conditioning

Following Pavlov's accidental discovery researchers made little progress on the learning process of animals until an American scientist, B.F. Skinner, took these early experiments much further using rats in a controlled environment. The caged rat was automatically given a pellet of food each time it pressed a lever attached to the dispenser until the rat had learned that the way to get food was to press the lever. Through certain variations on this theme, Skinner's experiments were able to accurately show that behaviour will not be learned if it is never rewarded (reinforced) to the benefit of the animal, but that same behaviour will soon become conditioned if it is rewarded (reinforced). He also found that the behaviour is more likely to continue if it is reinforced on an irregular basis and not every time. Perhaps the most important conclusion was that if a learned behaviour is never again reinforced, it will become unlearned.

Operant conditioning is the basis of all modern dog training, whereby the trainer is completely in control of teaching the dog new behaviours and eliminating undesirable behaviours by the use of stimuli and reinforcement, both positive and negative.

In human terms we can associate this with playing a slot machine. You would never play it again if it never paid out, but unfortunately we are conditioned to occasionally expect something in return for continuing to feed it money and there is the bigger lure of the ultimate reward, 'the jackpot'. If you got out exactly what you had just put in each time you pulled the lever then boredom would soon make you stop playing.

POSITIVE REINFORCEMENT

If, when a dog exhibits a certain behaviour, a stimulus is given which makes the behaviour more likely to occur again, *reinforcement* has taken place and the stimulus is actually the reinforcer.

For example, when your little puppy runs up to you and you immediately give it a titbit,

Dogs communicate in a different way.

you have reinforced it coming to you with a primary reinforcer – food. This behaviour of coming to you is now more likely to reoccur in the future. Now carrying an endless supply of treats is just not practical, and indeed once the puppy is full and the survival instinct of eating to avoid starvation has been satisfied the food will stop being an effective reinforcer and the desired behaviour may reduce.

So what are the alternatives? Saying 'Good boy!' to a dog actually means nothing at all unless these words have been conditioned to be a reinforcer.

Complicated? Not at all. Every time the puppy is given food, 'Good boy' is said at the same time until 'Good boy', which was a neutral stimulus, will now become a conditioned reinforcer. Puppies love being touched and stroked so this primary reinforcer of touch, like food, can also be used to condition 'Good boy' as a reinforcer. Of course the exact words used do not matter to the dog but it is easier, or rather less confusing for the trainer, to use words that the human brain can immediately associate with the action. The less we confuse ourselves, the less we will confuse our dogs!

So now we have some basic tools, which can be used to teach a dog to repeat a good behaviour. Reward for an action makes it happen again. This is simply the *positive reinforcement* of behaviour.

NEGATIVE REINFORCEMENT

The opposite, the removal of an unpleasant stimulus, can be just as effective to alter or teach certain behaviours. When a behaviour is strengthened by the removal of a negative stimulus (something unpleasant to the dog) this is termed negative reinforcement – for example, the release of a tight slip collar when the dog stops pulling on the lead.

This of course must not be confused with punishment, which decreases the chance of a behaviour happening again, but I admit there is a very close connection at times between the two. Another example of negative reinforcement is using pressure by pushing the hand on the dog's bottom to make it sit; the physical action of sitting removes the unpleasant pressure as the bottom is lowered, when the dog can be rewarded.

As in the latter example, negative reinforcement is usually closely followed by positive reinforcement of the correct behaviour that follows. The dog stops pulling to escape from the discomfort caused by the slip lead; this is immediately followed by praising the dog for the correct behaviour (walking on the slack lead). So now walking on a slack lead is more likely to reoccur in the future due to negative and positive reinforcement.

Many dogs do not like being ignored. Being pack animals, they find solitude unpleasant and so again this can be used as a negative reinforcer. I have many dogs that come in for residential training that really show no interest in their owners whatsoever, and are usually happy to disappear across the open fields when given the chance. This superficial self-confidence soon begins to diminish in the confines of this new pack environment where I am the established leader and the new arrival is unsure of its position. It may take several days before the unpleasantness of hiding in the kennel forces the newcomer out into the confines of the kennel yard; I will continue to go about my business until the unpleasantness of being ignored forces the dog to approach me, when I will immediately acknowledge this with a reward (positive reinforcement). Within a week or two the dog will seek my attention constantly, preferring this to isolation.

PUNISHMENT

This is something applied as a consequence for a behaviour, which makes it less likely to occur again. This does not necessarily mean something physical has to be administered, indeed a verbal reprimand using the words 'no', 'bad dog' or the harsh sound 'aagh' from the back of the throat, can all be used as punishers. However, be aware that although humans will understand the meaning of these verbal sounds, for them to be effective with the dog they must have been previously conditioned as punishers by associating the sound with something unpleasant. Much the same as 'Good boy' became a conditioned reinforcer, 'Bad boy' can be conditioned as a punisher.

Punishment is a valuable tool that I use sparingly during training, but this must not be confused with the cruel and unnecessary practices advocated by some. Punishment may just be the removal of something pleasant, like a dog's freedom to play, or the removal of the owner's attention or the correct use of a slip chain or slip lead to teach heelwork. It may be physical, such as gripping the loose skin each side of the neck, but should not be such that injury to the dog could result.

Punishment could also be simply the withholding of a reward until the dog does the task right – for example, if the dog turns its head away when presenting the dummy it is not rewarded, but when it delivers the dummy correctly, it is.

The most extreme forms of punishment involve electric shocks, beatings, pinch collars, ear biting and so on. None of these deserve a place in the modern training environment and they are mentioned here only to indicate how the word 'punishment' can be completely misinterpreted.

EXTINCTION

This is not what you think, or rather not what I thought when I read the term for the first time. It is the extinction of behaviours, not life, and usually it applies to unwanted problem behaviour that, through being ignored, or not reinforced, diminishes and eventually does no reoccur. A dog that jumps up at strangers will cease to do it if the behaviour is never reinforced.

Confused again because that does not work in all cases?

Well we all know that it is perhaps not quite so simple with a very sociable domesticated pack-loving animal, but let me remind you of what makes the behaviour reoccur. Reinforcement is a stimulus that, when associated with a behaviour, is likely to make that behaviour reoccur. Now the conflict comes; what is a 'reward' or 'reinforcer' to the dog is not necessarily considered a 'reward' to the trainer. A very social dog is quite happy to receive a shriek as a 'reward' for meeting and greeting with all four feet, even better if the shriek is associated with some human hands to play with or bite – and so the behaviour is reinforced, and will happen again in the future!

The extinction process can also happen to good behaviour if you fail to reinforce it at all. A dog taught to walk on a slack lead, using operant conditioning, will eventually begin to pull again if the good behaviour is never positively reinforced and the bad behaviour is subsequently allowed. However, I am not sure whether the reflex action of salivation of Pavlov's dogs on the sound of the bell produced by classical conditioning could have been halted using extinction, but in theory it should be possible.

TIMING

A reinforcement for a behaviour should be given at the exact point in time that the behaviour occurs. So when using positive reinforcement, the dog must easily associate the reward with the desired behaviour. To condition the 'stay', for example, it is no use calling the dog up from the stay and then rewarding, it as then the action of coming is being reinforced but the 'stay' is not; in that case the timing is incorrect.

The same applies equally to negative reinforcement or punishment, in that the reinforcement must be delivered at the exact time the unwanted behaviour occurs, so the dog associates it with the correct behaviour.

LINKING OR CHAINING

Many exercises that a dog does can be broken down into several different elements, so this term reflects the teaching of each of the individual elements (links) separately and then joining them all together into the final sequence (the chain). Retrieving a dummy, for example, consists of a sit, stay, watch and mark, out run, search, pick-up, return, sit, present, deliver and finish. All can be taught at different lessons before you link them all together.

CUES OR PROMPTS

A cue or prompt is a stimulus or circumstance that precedes the occurrence of a desired behaviour. It may be something that you do, for example a sound such as a verbal order or whistle command and a visual signal such as a raised hand to make the dog sit down. The use of the lead can also be a cue to walking nicely by your side. The environment can also provide its own cues to certain behaviours, such as using a narrow corridor to produce a straight return with a dummy.

FADING

This is the gradual reduction of a cue, i.e. a quieter whistle or verbal command, or the reduction of the associated commands so that the dog sits down on the whistle alone without the verbal command and hand signal.

Another example is the gradual removal of the use of the lead, as the dog is now walking nicely by your side.

The use of the environmental prompt, such as the narrow corridor to encourage a straight retrieve, is gradually reduced, or faded, so that when retrieving from open ground the straight return is maintained.

SHAPING

Do you remember playing 'hot or cold' as a child when searching for something that was

Gundogs correctly desensitized to loud bangs will not be afraid of gunshot, as demonstrated by Mick Harrison shooting clays over his yellow Labrador at the Saham Toney Charity Team Test in July 2006.

hidden by your playmates? They would shout 'Warmer!' or 'Colder!' depending on whether you were getting closer to the object or further away, and would shriek 'Very hot!' when you were almost there. This concept lies behind the use of 'shaping' during training; the dog is rewarded for any behaviour that is close to that which is ultimately required. By then reinforcing any successive behaviours we then gradually lead the dog closer to the one we require.

The 'sit', for instance, is first rewarded when the puppy is put into the sitting position by its handler, next the reward is only given when the dog does it to the command, then that is extended until the dog is sitting straight and only rewarded when looking up at the handler so that eye contact is conditioned.

FLOODING

This term means flooding the senses with objects that have a very strong attraction, or those that may cause a fear response, in order to overcome any unwanted behaviour toward the object.

An example of a fear response is a dog that is afraid of gunfire. To deal with this using the flooding approach, the dog might be taken to a clay shoot regularly, and kept on the lead so there is no escape from the noise. This may work in some cases, but it could also have a more devastating and long-lasting detrimental effect. Therefore for these hearing-based fear responses I would recommend systematic desensitization (below).

However, the neutral stimulus, the gun, may have actually been conditioned to be an object that creates a fear-based response. The fear of the actual weapon must first be overcome, and this *can* be achieved by flooding. Leave the weapon hanging in the same room or kennel with the dog, where there is no escape, until it no longer pays any attention to it. Carry it with you at all times when out for daily walks, feed the dog with the gun lying by the bowl, and as the gun becomes an integral part of daily life over a few weeks the next stage, to overcome the fear response to the bang, should be simplified.

SYSTEMATIC DESENSITIZATION

This process uses several gradual stages to get the dog to overcome, or counter-conditioned to, a fear or phobia. If we look at the fear of the gunshot, this very often is coupled with a fear of the actual weapon through its previous association with the noise, and the fear of the gun must be dealt with first by flooding.

When using desensitization, on no account must the fear reaction be rewarded with coaxing or cajoling. The art is to make the different stages so gradual that the fear reaction does not happen and correct behaviour can be rewarded.

HABITUATION

This technique gets a dog used to an occurrence that may have been the cause of a negative reaction when first encountered, by being exposed to it several times.

In the shooting field it is not uncommon for a young dog to be startled by or show fear of an object like a feed hopper the first time it is suddenly confronted with it. The youngster may jump back, tail down, hackles raised, possibly accompanied by a muffled bark or two. If you subsequently walk or work the dog near this strange object on several occasions, the dog will soon become habituated to the object and so the reaction will disappear. I have seen the same reaction when a puppy meets a hedgehog for the first time on the garden lawn or comes across a plastic bag fluttering in the wind.

If a young dog that has not been exposed to game before is found to be very keen with live game, to the point where this fascination is so intense that it completely disregards its handler when game is present, then controlled exposure to watching game all day, every day, will eventually reduce this latent fascination.

COUNTER-CONDITIONING

This approach does exactly what it says on the tin – it counters, or undoes, the usually adverse effects that have been caused by previous conditioning.

If, for example, the dog only takes the sitting position on the third command to 'sit', it will be taught using counter-conditioning to sit on the first command. This is done by enforcing and then reinforcing the correct behaviour.

CONCLUSION

This chapter will, I hope, have given you a deeper understanding of the way that dogs learn. Remembering the following points will help you when training your dog:

- A behaviour associated with a reward will make that behaviour more likely to reoccur and, through the repetition of this behaviour in association with a command and the subsequent reward, conditioning will take place.
- A behaviour that is punished, associated with something unpleasant or not rewarded will be less likely to reoccur.
- We have the power to analyse situations that happen during training, but the dog does not so the onus is on us to be clear and fair, and to avoid confusion. This will help our dogs to achieve the high level of control that we are aiming for.
- Please do remember that a 'reward' to a dog is something that the dog wants, and this may often be contrary to what you the trainer thinks is a 'reward'.

Please refer back to this chapter whenever the learning process appears not to be working.

CHAPTER THREE

Training the Trainer

The importance of choosing the right training environment for you and your dog. The pros and cons of class training and of one-to-one lessons, and the importance of correct and appropriate training for the human trainee, as well as the canine.

INSTRUCTING, NOT TRAINING

The concept of teaching someone else to do a task is much more involved than directly doing the task yourself. This is even more complex in dog training, when you are dealing both with the human mind and the canine mind. It may seem easy for me in my role of instructor to explain to the person how to do the same things that I as the trainer would do, and for them to be able to achieve the same results as myself, but in reality that is very far from the truth.

It is important for me as the instructor to assess the physical and mental abilities of the human pupil who I am going to develop into a dog trainer at the same time as assessing the ability of their dog. The dog, of course, with the right guidance from me to the trainer, is going to develop into an obedient companion and, if necessary, a competent gundog. I have spent many frustrating hours over at least two decades in this role of an instructor concentrating on developing other people's training skills but I have in the process also been gaining further instructing skills of my own. I now always gain a great sense of achievement each time one of my pupils makes progress and succeeds at what they are doing, no matter how small that progress may seem to others. I know that with each step forward the confidence of my pupil will grow, and that will help develop their ability to learn even more and pass what they have learned onto their canine companion.

ONE-TO-ONE VERSUS CLASS LESSONS

I am a great believer in one-to-one lessons, as opposed to classes, as they enable full concentration to be maintained by the pupil, their dog and, importantly, the instructor. The regular class situation, although it can be of great benefit to some, does become more complex for the instructor when trying to deal with individual problems. The bigger the class, the more chance there is that learning will not be achieved by many of the attendees. Untrained dogs do not behave well in company; they may show fear or aggression, or be disruptive and noisy through having been previously over-socialized. In the case of male dogs this disruptive behaviour may be because they are more interested in the ladies; indeed all these things can apply to their owners too!

The author as a KCAI Instructor, giving guidance on dog training.

I will deal separately with these two different ways of teaching people to be able to train their dogs, to enable a clearer understanding to be gained by both the aspiring instructor of people and the aspiring trainer of dogs.

Classes

Being confronted with a class of up to a dozen new faces and different breeds of gundog of which the instructor has no intimate knowledge can be a daunting prospect. If the class instructor is not thoroughly prepared then the chance of all those people and dogs still being there as the course of lessons comes to a conclusion in a few months' time is remote. With the best will in the world some of them will not achieve success or fulfil their own expectations and they may soon become disillusioned. Good instructors should run the class to suit all their pupils' needs.

I have in the past spent an hour talking about and demonstrating my particular training skills and methods to a gundog training class with the intention that those class pupils can go home at the end, armed with all the newly acquired knowledge, to subsequently train their dogs before the next lesson in a couple of weeks' time. However, I commonly find that when some of them return for the next lesson they are no further forward. This is usually due to a total lack of understanding or recollection of what I showed them on the previous occasion.

Although it would be easy to blame them for not paying attention, this is not always the reason for a lack of progress. It may be that for whatever reason my methods of instructing were not particularly captivating during that particular lesson. Having said that, experience has taught me that there are an increasing number of people who enjoy going to public classes just to be part of the scene and to socialize, rather than having any intention of learning. This is much the same as people who are bored with their lives finding an adult education course that is of no practical use to

Anthea Lawrence, KCAI Instructor, running a class for Golden Retrievers, and ensuring it is a positive learning experience.

them at all other than getting out of the house once or twice a week. These social people are usually really nice, but their attitude can distract the attention of those who genuinely want to learn how to train their dog.

Disadvantages of Class Teaching

Let's look at some of the reasons why classes can create problems or blocks to learning for those potential dog trainers who are genuinely there to be educated.

People can learn the theory by reading, watching or listening, then put what they have learned into practice later. However, to ensure the lesson has been interpreted correctly by the pupil it is better if they are allowed to have a go at the time, and subsequently keep trying and practising whilst under the close supervision of the instructor so that guidance can be given. The amount of time under guidance and the amount of practice to make perfect is dependent on the aptitude of the trainer and, of course, the learning ability of the particular dog that they are trying to train.

Many people who attend dog training classes have not been involved in any form of education for many years, and may have forgotten the process of how to learn or remember, or may just lack confidence in their own ability. I never liked the formality of schoolroom lessons, and was far more attentive when taught something in a more relaxed way, such as rugby out on the sports field. The formality I remember from grammar school can still exist in some dog training classes.

A person who is lacking confidence will immediately feel under pressure when put in a class with people who have a greater understanding of the subject, or with those who are more outgoing. So this less confident person will probably allow the others in the class to keep taking the lead, as they will be more preoccupied with the pressures on them rather than having a go or listening to the instructor's words of wisdom.

Some class members may already have preconceived ideas on how they should train their dog; they will probably overestimate their own ability and be reluctant to accept a new approach. This will cause conflict if the

The instructor should ask questions to retain attention and to keep communication alive.

instructor does not take a flexible approach. A good method of training a dog to do a particular task is the one that works for the dog, from the many ways on offer, as long as the dog's welfare is not compromised in any way through harsh handling.

Less confident class members will appreciate being told by the instructor when they are doing well. Conversely, however, they will not be encouraged by continually making self-comparisons with the other class members, many of whom may appear to be advancing much more quickly.

In the same way that individual dogs learn in different ways and at different speeds, the owners will too. There is not one blueprint for teaching a dog, and the same is true of people; they will each need to be assessed and then taught in a way that the individual pupil can relate to and so absorb knowledge at a comfortable rate.

There are occasions when a person in the class needs individual instruction, and even those instructors who only run group training classes will admit they have to sometimes spend time separately with this type of individual either during the class or perhaps immediately afterwards. This can cause further learning problems as, now that an individual is receiving special treatment, other class members who have not had this service made available to them may get upset. The fact they probably do not need it is, to some, irrelevant. It really is a job to please everyone all of the time in the dog game!

Gary Vidler gives a pupil individual instruction during a demonstration on the use of the new Dummy Shot.

How to Create a Positive Environment

The instructor who is arranging classes or one-to-one lessons must try to provide an environment that is beneficial to the learning process and so avoid some of the above problems from occurring. The classes must be able to fulfil every pupil's expectations, but of course each one of them will have different expectations. So a good assessment of each individual and their dog before putting them into the class situation is essential.

Treat everyone from the start as an individual, but make sure they are all fully integrated into the class and into all the activities of the lesson. Everyone in the class should be treated with the same respect, whether young or old.

Make sure that everyone enters into any discussion periods; if they do not join in willingly, they need to be gently encouraged to take part fully.

Every member of that class needs to feel at ease, and they also need to feel secure. An open field may be great later on, but for the nervous person with a dog that they already know can seek independence, if given the opportunity, it would be a very unnerving environment.

Each pupil must know at all times what is expected of them and they must all take part in what is going on in each lesson. Continual monitoring and assessment of progress by the instructor will enable each individual to be kept informed on exactly how they are progressing, without there being any grading or comparison with the achievements of other class members.

To make sure the communication process is working, and to retain attention, the instructor should ask questions from time to time to ensure that every individual has heard correctly and so has fully grasped what the lesson is actually about.

If the learning environment has a positive influence on the pupil then they are more likely to achieve. However, if a pupil is made to feel inadequate, because they are not advancing as fast as the others, or because they are old or immature, or because they have an unusual breed of dog, negativity will set in and a severe block to their learning will be the result.

One-to-One Training

In my experience, the problems and subsequent blocks to learning that are likely to be encountered in a public class do not happen very often with one-to-one lessons. Pupils have the undivided attention of their instructor, and as soon as something needs attention or their concentration waivers, or if they start chattering about something totally irrelevant to the particular part of the lesson, they can be immediately steered back in the right direction.

Every person learns in a different way. One-to-one training allows a trainer to tailor and deliver each lesson to suit the individual's learning ability. When we were being taught in large classes at school, we were not given individual tuition and were expected to digest the teaching in the same way. My form master did not take into account that we could not all commit complicated formulas to memory after being shown them once on the blackboard. Some of us did need to see them over and over again, whilst for others just by hearing the lesson once they acquired the knowledge immediately. I found that the practical application of the theory I had previously learned parrot-fashion was the only way to consolidate my understanding of it and commit it to memory. The same is true of dog training; whether the theory has been fully learned or not, success is only achievable once it has been properly put into practice, resulting in a well-trained canine companion with, most importantly, a competent handler.

The canine part of the partnership under instruction is very often a 'clean sheet'. It is the handler who usually comes with all sorts of baggage and preconceived ideas of what is going to happen. It is important that the instructor can assess the client accurately so that the learning process proceeds at the correct speed and at the right depth. If too much detail is given too quickly the handler may be overwhelmed, and a lack of understanding will result. The first few lessons are particularly important as they give the instructor an opportunity to build a good relationship between them and the handler. Any breakdown in the communication process will discourage this from happening.

CONCLUSION

Whilst this book is primarily about you training the dog, you are the person that is going to do it and the training therefore needs to be learned by you, before you can teach the dog. It is therefore useful to have knowledge of the human learning process as well.

As a Kennel Club Accredited Instructor (KCAI) I am fully aware of the difficulties that people new to this art can experience. If the trainer gives up through a lack of understanding then their dog's training will probably not be finished and there could be all sorts of problems for the family to endure in the years ahead.

CHAPTER FOUR

Prepare for the Next Eighteen Months

How to prepare for your puppy's arrival. Health, feeding and early checks. The uses, and merits, of the practical training aids that are available, as well as a number that can be made at home. The correct use of commands, together with the author's own commands. The pros and cons of DIY training and professional residential training for the young gundog.

THE NEW ARRIVAL

Your gundog may be only eight weeks old when you collect it from the breeder. You will be wise to be fully prepared for its arrival in advance. Make sure that you receive all of its documents, together with details of worming or vaccinations and of course its present feeding regime. Take something secure and comfortable to transport it home in the car or, if preferred, a towel to put on your lap in case of little accidents. Its immediate care and welfare are of paramount importance for its smooth transition from being a puppy into a fully integrated part of the family home and a competent shooting companion. Even if it is an adolescent, or older, it will still need settling into the new home environment carefully, particularly if all its early life was spent in kennels.

Health and Welfare

The new puppy must have its own warm, dry, secure place where it can retreat to rest or sleep. This may be a purpose-built kennel and run outside in the garden with its own snug sleeping quarters, or it may be a space in the family home. If the latter, then it must be chosen carefully so that the new puppy can adjust and feel secure in this strange environment as quickly as possible. A utility room is a common choice, but as puppies do chew when bored all electrical appliances must be well protected. Equally, the puppy being woken up by the washing machine starting with the economy 7 tariff at midnight may be very upsetting for it, and its vocal remonstrations could soon wake the whole household. The conservatory is used by some as a dog room, but this gets too hot in summer and dogs have been known to cruelly perish in the same way as if they had been left enclosed in a car.

Phil and Christina Wade collecting Ormewood Oliver, complete with documents, food and 'new puppy' guide.

A comfortable bed is a must considering the puppy has just left the warmth of its siblings in the nest. Ready access to fresh water, preferably in a spill- and chew-proof bowl, is also essential and, of course, after drinking it will need to answer a call of nature until house-training and conditioned self-control have been established. The dead of night can be very quiet and so a ticking clock or, better still, a radio left on will help the puppy feel less isolated and less likely to start howling for attention. A large knuckle-bone will also distract and occupy it if it is awoken during the night, especially for the weeks when it is enduring the discomfort of teething.

Feeding

The breeder should have supplied details of your puppy's current feeding regime, but that does not mean you must stick rigidly to it. There are a multitude of excellent complete dry foods available, although I prefer to add raw meat or offal, such as fresh tripe, to the diet until my puppies are 4 or 5 months old. If I only had one or two to rear then I would consider the BARF (bones and raw food) diet, which produces excellent results if a reliable source of the necessary products can be secured and subsequently kept in hygienic conditions.

Veterinary Check

Registration with a local veterinary practice is essential, and it is a good idea if you are new to dog ownership to make an appointment for the first week after obtaining your new puppy so that any health problems can be immediately identified or diagnosed. Although small puppies carry a certain amount of immunity from the mother they do need the added protection afforded by vaccination against some really nasty canine diseases. Your vet will be able to advise on these and, of course, on regular worming and treatment for skin parasites such as fleas, lice or ticks. This is also a good time to consider 'identichipping' the puppy just in case it is lost or, worst still, stolen in the future. Until the puppy has been fully immunized it should, of course, not be allowed to come into contact with other dogs in public areas.

PRACTICAL TRAINING AIDS

I have a varied array of different training aids collected over a long period of time in my store, many of which are just novelties now gathering dust. Many of these artificial aids are unnecessary, and I find the less that are used to train a gundog the better. After all, the shooting man only wants a dog that is biddable and that will walk steadily at heel or hunt comfortably within range of the gun. There is little necessity for the dog to be able to mark, locate and retrieve a plastic dummy launched excessive distances. However, used carefully many of the traditional and modern artificial aids can make a useful contribution to a dog's training.

A selection of training aids. Top row, left to right: rabbit skin dummy, standard canvas dummy, puppy canvas dummy, tennis ball thrower, squeaky pheasant dog toy, rubber teal, rubber mallard. Middle row, left to right: child's tennis racket and balls, white launcher dummy, dummy launcher and black dummy, coney fur dummy, dried pheasant, partridge, pigeon wings. Bottom row, left to right: sock dummy, with Kong toy above, ragger, partridge and duck wings for use on dummies.

Dummy Launchers

A hand-held dummy launcher sensibly used, particularly as an aid to steadiness or just to introduce a shot, may be an asset but at approximately £65 to £75 plus the additional cost of extra dummies and blanks they are not cheap. However, for the person who is unable to throw an ordinary dummy successfully they can be a boon.

I would advise anyone who is using a dummy launcher to train a young spaniel, to reduce the distance that the dummy is projected by not pushing it fully home onto the launcher. The same rule applies for the other breeds when using it for the first few lessons, until your dog is proficient at watching the dummy disappear at speed into the distance.

The dummy launcher is not a toy, and because it launches a relatively hard projectile it can be potentially very dangerous in the wrong hands. Wrist injury can also occur if the launcher is not held correctly or if it is not kept clean and well lubricated to reduce recoil. Firing, especially without the dummy attached, can produce a very loud noise that, besides upsetting the puppy, could also damage the user's ears. Therefore hearing protection should always be worn and the device should never be discharged directly over a dog's head.

Twelve-gauge snap caps modified for use with cartridge primers.

Hand-Throwing Dummies

I personally find standard-size canvas hand-throwing dummies to be more than adequate for the majority of situations that I wish to create for my pupils; this includes steadiness as well as retrieving. For the initial introduction, or for puppies or dogs that are reluctant retrievers, smaller dummies are a boon. Gradually these can be increased in size as the dog becomes more proficient. The addition of cured rabbit fur or dried game bird wings adds extra appeal and realism when required later in the training course.

Rabbit Fur and Wings

These are available from any good gundog training equipment supplier, but they can also be prepared at home. Wings removed from dead game can either be dried in a cool place protected from flies and moths, or just left in the freezer. They will need to be securely attached to the dummy with strong twine or elastic bands.

With a little skill a rabbit skin can be removed whole from a fresh carcass by making an incision along the back of the rear legs and gradually pulling it forward off the body in a tube. The skin, which is now flesh side out, can be cut free around the neck. This end of the tube is securely tied before rubbing the exposed underside with a liberal amount of salt and then rolling it back over a standard sized dummy to reveal the fur on the outside. The open end is then stitched closed, leaving the throwing string and toggle protruding. This dummy can be used immediately, but I prefer to let it hang in an airy place for several weeks before use, when it will shrink and grip the dummy firmly as it dries and any adverse odour will have abated.

Sock Dummies

These are easily made to any size. An outer sock is stuffed with more old socks or other soft material, and with a little skill the centre can be made narrower to help teach the puppy to balance it correctly. I find the sock dummy a boon when teaching the 'hold' to the reluctant retriever, and it is certainly more appealing than canvas.

Rubber Ducks

No, not the sort you play with in the bath, but those purpose-made in the USA to simulate the real thing from small teal through all the other types up to the size of a goose. The head and feet are made of very hard plastic and so the dog soon learns to pick the duck up correctly by its softer middle. The head is also joined to the body by cord so that if the dog has a tendency to shake the object, the head will smack it on the nose. Personally I have never trained a gundog with this dummy-shaking problem, but I am assured by a visitor from over the water that the dummy will stop shaking re-occurring.

Tennis Balls

These are invaluable; half a dozen can be carried quite easily in the pocket and they have a vast amount of different uses. With the aid of a small racket they can be accurately sent some distance further than if just thrown by hand. An attachment for firing tennis balls from a dummy launcher is also now available and the realism of a shot can then be directly associated with the retrieve. They will disappear out of sight into the lightest of cover and will encourage a young dog to use its nose to locate it rather than its eyes.

Simulated Gunfire

A gradual introduction to the sound of a shot to stop the trainee's motion if it's hunting, or to direct its eyes in the direction of the noise so enabling it to mark the retrieve, can be easily simulated in varying degrees of severity, but only after you are sure that the puppy shows no fear of noise at other times. Start with a simple clap of the hands, then the sound of an unloaded airgun being discharged, a starting pistol, dummy launcher, shotgun blank adapter and eventually the real thing, perhaps graduating from a 410 up to a twelve bore and even larger if the dog is to be used for shooting wildfowl on the foreshore.

A shotgun blank adapter can be bought which fires rimfire blanks as used in a dummy launcher, or alternatively one that fires primers as used in shotgun cartridges can be easily made from some twelve-gauge snap caps by removing the hard rubber centre that is normally used to cushion the firing pin when the spring is released prior to storing a shotgun. I prefer the latter type, as the primers are readily available and they are designed for a normal shotgun cartridge and so are less likely to damage the firing pins. Besides that, they do not jam in the adapters after being discharged like rimfire blanks definitely do.

Steadiness Aids

Steadiness is an essential quality in any well-trained dog; even the family pet should be taught self-control and be free of the desire to chase other animals and livestock, if social harmony is to be maintained during exercise in the town park or country fields alike. Equally, a well-trained gundog is expected to exercise self-control and only retrieve when directed by the handler, so should be taught not to run in to thrown objects or moving game.

The Elasticated Rabbit

For the person who does not have ready access to a rabbit pen, an elasticated rabbit can help them introduce their youngster to dropping to a simulated flush and will lay the seeds of steadiness to the real thing. With care the dummy rabbit can be twitched across the ground by a third party to really tease the puppy, but a pet rabbit hopping around is obviously far more tempting.

Elasticated rabbits can be very dangerous if the anchor spike is not firmly embedded in the ground. In my early impetuous gundog training years I had several near misses when the spike gave way in soft soil and came whistling passed my ear as I was stretching the elastic to its limit. The elastic itself can give you a very nasty smack when it breaks through normal wear and tear or after being stored in a damp place when it will soon perish. Take great care when using this equipment.

Remote control pigeon release trap set.

Remote control pigeon release trap sprung.

Battery-Operated Rabbit

I recently saw an old portable battery-operated rabbit, which had once belonged to a very successful field trial trainer of spaniels and retrievers, although I believe it belonged to a whippet trainer first. The dummy rabbit, being attached to the end of a long cord, could be wound in by the motor at varying speeds with occasional pauses to add realism and temptation; it could also be easily utilized for laying scent lines. The unit itself was quite cumbersome and I am surprised in this age of computer technology that a remote controlled fully transportable unit is not yet available.

Pigeon Release Traps

Electronically controlled, live pigeon release traps are also now readily available, at a price! You may have seen them successfully used at the Game Fair. They can be activated either manually by the use of a pull cord, or electronically using the radio remote control.

Identity tags are a requirement of the law when the dog is in a public place.

When activated these spring-loaded traps project the pigeon a foot or two up into the air, ensuring its safe escape from a keen young gundog, and the birds used will happily fly back to the loft completely unharmed and none the worse for their experience.

Live Rabbits

With common sense any of the previously mentioned artificial aids can assist the trainer towards achieving complete steadiness in their pupil, but once all this simulated work has been completed there is no substitute for the real thing to complete this part of a gundog puppy's training. A tame rabbit in the garden is helpful, but access to a large pen full of wild rabbits where steadiness can be taught in controlled conditions is by far superior.

Collars and Leads

Once the dog is trained a handy slip lead made from leather or rope should be adequate for general use, but it may not be suitable for easily teaching obedience and heelwork. At all times when the dog is not working but is off the lead in a public place it should wear a collar with an identity tag attached to satisfy the requirements of the law. Only when actually at work are sporting dogs exempt from this requirement.

I find a slip lead or heavy link chain preferable to a collar and lead when teaching heelwork for several reasons. They can be quickly removed and replaced without much delay when progressing to off-lead work whereas collars tend to be more fiddly. A slip lead or chain if jerked tightens around the dog's neck but the pressure releases immediately the lead goes slack. However, a collar only puts pressure on the front of the dog's throat, which is more uncomfortable and liable to cause it to gag or cough.

If the dog is strong and a slip chain is required then I only use heavy stainless steel chains with 1in (2.5cm) oval links of a size that gives ample slack when fitted round the dog's neck. Use a 30in (75cm) chain for a Labrador

A rope slip lead, correctly worn, will remain slack and comfortable.

and a 24in (60cm) chain for a spaniel as a rough guide. To avoid discomfort to the user the lead that is attached should be made from good quality harness leather and at least 4ft 6in (1.4m) long. Most commercially produced slip leads are too short, resulting in constant pressure being felt at the business end, but it is easy to join two together for the purposes of the training environment.

Whistles

I had just finished a public demonstration a few years ago when a very nice lady came up to me and asked about my whistle and where I bought it from. I explained that I was using a black plastic Acme 210½ without a pea and she immediately exclaimed, 'That's the same as mine, but mine doesn't work!' 'Perhaps it's faulty or blocked with debris?' I replied. However, she quickly went on to explain that her whistle did make a sound just like mine, but her dog apparently could not hear it, and certainly did not stop when she blew it!

Whistles do not work magic; your dog must be conditioned to respond to the sound of your whistle just like they are taught any other of your commands, whether verbal or physical. However, it is as well to practise blowing it correctly before trying to teach the dog to respond. I find that a sharper, more consistent sound is made if the whistle is blown in the same manner as playing a recorder. I use the tip of the tongue to block the mouthpiece until the air pressure in my mouth is sufficient; the quick removal of the tongue then allows the sound to be immediately and precisely delivered.

I personally recommend the black plastic whistle, which is the easiest to obtain and replace with an identical one should you lose it or, more likely if you enter competitions, chew the end to destruction. They come in several different pitches identified by the code number stamped on the underside. Some have a pea in, which makes a much sharper sound, but I avoid them and the thunderer type, which is more at home on the football pitch. Small stainless steel silent whistles can be tuned to the desired pitch and then locked with a small grub screw, but being metal the mouthpiece can freeze on the lips in very cold weather and over time will wear the front teeth of the user much like the pipe-smokers of old. Stag and buffalo horn whistles are expensive and vary greatly in pitch. Again, the final choice is up to the individual and the method of teaching the dog to respond to whatever one you choose will not change.

COMMANDS

As with the artificial aids, you will need to be prepared with a list of verbal commands that you in turn will teach the dog to react to. The very same thought process applies with verbal commands as it does the whistle – you cannot keep experimenting with different words, hoping that one will eventually work. You need to be confident and consistent to teach your dog the words of command and the specific way it must respond to them. I try to keep the same set of verbal commands for all the trainees, whether my own or my clients', so that I am less likely to make a mistake and add confusion by using something different.

A word about choosing your dog's name. The only sound that is individual to each dog is, of

Author's list of commands

Action Required	Voice Command	Whistle	Hand Signal
To sit	'Sit'	Single blast	Open flat palm
To walk by handler's side	'Heel'	n/a	Slap left thigh
To remain in one place	'Stay'	n/a	Open flat palm
To come back (recall)	'Here'	Series of pips	Open arms and slap legs
To go for marked retrieve	'Fetch it'	n/a	Point in direction
To go for unseen or push back and away	'Get out'	n/a	Point in direction
To set off hunting	'Gone away'	n/a	Cast hand in direction required
To stop when hunting or to re-direct	'Sit'	Single blast	Open flat palm
To change direction	'Sit'	Single blast	Throw arm in the direction required
To search an area for retrieve	'There'	n/a	n/a
To release dummy/game to hand	'Dead'	n/a	n/a
Not to pick up (carcass perhaps)	'Leave'	n/a	n/a
To go in kennel, trailer or car	'Kennel'	n/a	Point in direction required

course, its name. Bearing in mind its use when working in the shooting field, several factors should influence the choice. Try to avoid anything that is likely to be confused with one of the command words. I recently helped a client who had a Labrador called 'Tia' and, although this name starts with a 'T', confusion was apparent when the dog was taught the chosen recall command of 'Here', especially if it was a windy day when the two words sounded identical at a distance. A single or double syllable short name is preferable, and if the dog is trained to react to it properly you should never feel the need to add an expletive in front of it when things do sometimes go wrong!

Although the dog's name is one of the first things you decide upon, it is as well to list your verbal command words before choosing the name so that a possible clash with the chosen name is avoided. My own verbal commands are listed on the previous page, together with the associated hand signals and whistle commands, and the expected behaviour/action by the dog to show how all these link together.

The commands listed are all ones that require a definite response from the dog. I do of course use other verbal noises or words, which mean 'Stop doing that immediately' or 'I do not like what you are doing.' So 'No' and/or 'Aagh' are used as punishers, delivered in a deep gruff tone.

The vocabulary of command words are not all used the moment I begin a puppy's training. Instead each one is introduced gradually during the training process. Some are easy to teach by direct association with a reward, such as the dog's name, but be careful not to begin to use its name in a different tone as a punisher should the dog do wrong (hence the suggested use of 'Aagh' or 'No' instead). Other commands will take considerable time and repetition before the dog really grasps their use. The search command 'There' is a prime example where the reward for doing it right is finding the retrieve, but because of the distance between dog and handler it can take a long time to perfect.

It is also important that if you are teaching a dog to obey every command it should respond to each different vocal, whistle and visible signal individually as well as when they are used collectively.

REWARDS

This is the more common term used to describe positive reinforcers, which when used correctly will ensure that the behaviour that was reinforced is more likely to happen again. I do not personally use titbits for training dogs in obedience or field work; however, I do use them around the kennels and home to encourage good behaviour in certain circumstances. Many puppies eventually stop going easily to their bed, whether it be in a kennel or a room in the house as they reach adolescence. This rebellion will be less likely to arise if they are rewarded for going straight in by finding food of some description already waiting within.

Praise

When conducting more formal training I prefer to use praise and touch to reinforce good behaviour. The meaning of the phrase 'Good boy!' is obvious to the human mind but means nothing to a canine. It has to be conditioned as a reinforcer by its association with something pleasant and then it becomes a powerful tool that can be delivered at a distance.

Touch

Touch definitely means something pleasurable to a dog immediately it is used, but it needs to be carried out correctly if it is going to be established as a reward. I use very gentle touch to induce calmness in the puppy, stroking in a circular motion either the chest or the back of the head with the tips of my fingers. If done properly the pup will close its eyes and relax as the gentle massage is delivered. I then know that it is definitely enjoying its reward.

Rough stroking would tend to encourage boisterous behaviour, so it must be avoided right from the start of rearing.

DIY TRAINING

Training a gundog for the first time can be very rewarding, but equally very frustrating when things go wrong. I remember working my way methodically through as many books as I could lay my hands on but failing to grasp the importance of instilling strict obedience whilst forming a close bond with the puppy right from the beginning of the relationship. I fell into the same trap as many others, rushing impetuously forward to the more interesting aspects of hunting, game and shooting before the training was complete. I also armed myself with all the latest gimmicks and the results were two independent hard-hunting liabilities and, on more than one occasion, a very red face. The first disaster was the yellow Labrador Sadi, from show lines, who was unstoppable when on scent but brilliant at putting game in the bag from absolutely vast distances. I do not think you would find such a physically proficient Labrador from completely show stock in the modern day. The second was the very difficult dishonest little liver and white Cocker bitch, Katy, but I am positive that in experienced hands they both would have made top class working dogs.

There is no blueprint for dog training; all successful professionals and amateurs alike have varying methods, but the finished article should be similar – a biddable, trustworthy companion that is a pleasure to own, both at home and in the shooting field.

Time is a very important commodity during training, little and often being the key to success. It is no good attending a gundog training class for a couple of hours once a fortnight and then doing nothing in between; ten- to fifteen-minute lessons once or twice every day are required to maintain the learning process at a satisfactory rate, especially during early obedience training.

If you need help or advice then good training classes for retrievers are relatively easy to find, but for spaniels and the other breeds they are few and far between. The Kennel Club maintains a list of all dog training clubs.

PERSONAL TUITION

You may wish to consider personal tuition as an alternative to going it alone, but beware, there seems to be an upsurge in the instant professional instructors, some of whom charge huge amounts of money just because they have included the word 'Behaviourist' after their name. At the present time there is no official licensing or control of these people and they may be only too willing to help you part with your money under false pretences. Of course those of us who have been through the rigorous KCAI scheme are accountable and abide by the Kennel Club Code of Practice.

The only real measure of another person's ability to train a working gundog must be their previous success with the dogs they have personally trained and handled in field trial competitions. Any bona fide trainer will be pleased to put your mind at rest in this respect by showing you the certificates they have gained as proof, though that does not always mean they are competent as an instructor to teach you the art of doing it yourself.

RESIDENTIAL TRAINING

The true professional who takes gundogs in for training will be fully geared up, with all the equipment necessary to take the client's dog right through the full training course to the finished article, even giving experience in the shooting field if required. People in this modern world do not always have the time to devote to early training and so once the puppy has been well socialized it may be worth considering sending it away for a month or two to have it taught the basics. Some personal lessons afterwards with the trainer and the puppy should put you both well on the track to continued success, but you will still need to equip yourself with the necessary aids to maintain the training once it comes back home.

'Not a Field Trial Dog'

When discussing a dog's training requirements I so often hear the comment 'but I do

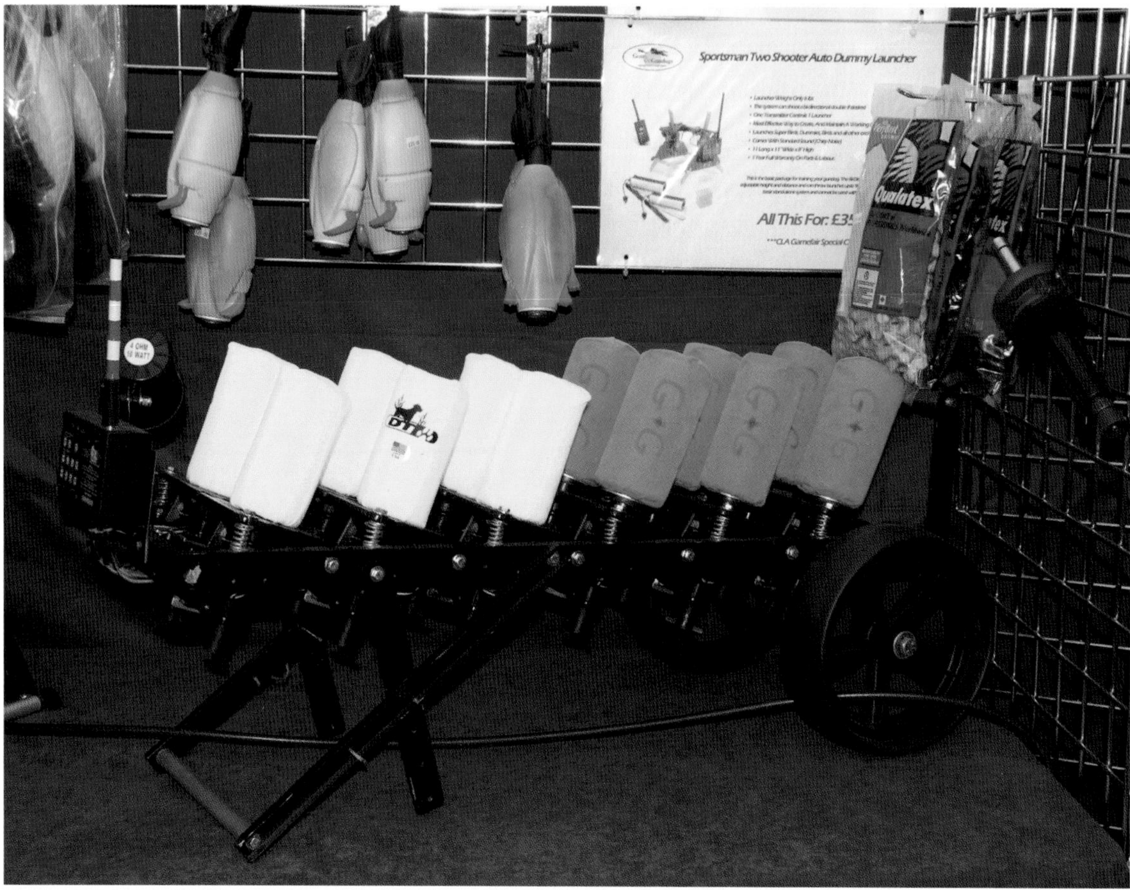

Expensive gimmick or necessary equipment?

not want a field trial dog'. When asked what they do want, the owner's response is usually not far removed from a description of exactly that. A field trial dog is just a well-trained, biddable gundog but it is born with that little bit extra style, drive and the 'wow' factor necessary to win in competition. Unless specifically asked to bring out these extra qualities, most professionals will do their utmost to produce a calm, steady, easily controlled companion for their clients.

I do not wish to deter anyone who is intent on training a gundog themselves for the first time, but before starting out make sure that you will be able to devote the necessary time to the task and, more importantly, if problems arise do not be afraid to seek out proper help quickly.

Rabbit Pen Work

Certain parts of a training course cannot be completed without access to a rabbit pen or other game supply in a controlled environment. For the more determined trainee perhaps a week or two away at this time will pay dividends. Your new gundog may be your only shooting dog for the next decade, and if you are going to enjoy its company for all of that time then, for the first couple of years, correct training and experience on the real thing are crucial.

Prepare for its Return Home

Having reared your puppy from the nest to adolescence you may have decided that DIY training was not for you, and that training by a professional was the best option for your

The owner should be given a complete practical demonstration of their dog's training progress.

puppy to learn his basic obedience, or even to complete his formal training to the gun. You will still need to prepare yourself with some of the equipment described when the puppy returns, so that the training is maintained. Even if basic obedience training only was required then the dog will have been away to gundog 'school' for several weeks, in which time it will have built a strong bond with its new, temporary master. Do not be disappointed or surprised when you eventually go to collect the dog if it ignores you completely at first. I personally would worry if the trainer had not got the puppy's undivided attention after going through the training course.

Demonstration

The trainer should not only now demonstrate your puppy's progress but should also explain the various commands, actions and equipment required to enable you to handle your dog correctly, and hopefully avoid a breakdown in discipline once the dog is back under your guardianship. You should also be provided with a written summary of commands and other useful information to help you maintain continuity with the training methods used by the trainer.

Do not be afraid to ask questions if you are not sure of any particular aspect – a clear understanding of these controls is required if you are to progress without undoing weeks of the trainer's hard work and also the possibility of incurring more expense in the future. Make a particular note of the commands used, paying attention to the professional's changes in tone, whistle and voice commands so that you may try to emulate him when handling your dog in the future.

The Dog's Subsequent Management

Although your dog may have been through a full course of training and is ready for shooting experience, *do not* take it out with the gun for several weeks until you are able to handle the dog confidently under ideal training conditions. On the pupil's first arrival back home it should be settled in again carefully – you need to establish a close bond with the dog similar to that it has enjoyed with the trainer.

The dog has got used to a completely different environment and management regime in the period away at boarding school. So it needs to feel very secure and happy before you think about attempting to handle it out in the field. Although you may be very keen to test the new skills that it has been taught it is better to be patient and allow it to adjust to the change of environment for a couple of weeks. You need to earn the dog's respect and confidence for success to follow. Assuming that this is your first experience of handling a trained gundog, you will need to gain confidence in your own ability to exercise control also. You must progress slowly through the different aspects of gundog work together now so that a lifelong harmonious partnership will be the end result.

PART-TRAINED

Many aspiring amateurs, although able to complete the training and then expertly handle their gundog in the shooting field, are unable to instil basic obedience, which is of course the foundation stone of any further education.

The Basics

The basic obedience course for any well-bred young gundog of around six to twelve months old, and from working stock, can be taught in six to eight weeks, at the end of which the puppy should be obedient both on and off the lead, understanding and responding confidently to the 'Sit', 'Stay', 'Here' and 'Heel' commands.

For some people, sending a dog to a trainer who will teach them the basics will certainly be money well spent, as many of the problems I deal with for clients with older dogs can be attributed to a deficiency in the animal's basic training. Often the only solution is to start at the beginning again, to improve or hopefully put matters right.

With the basic commands having been taught professionally you will now be able to progress more rapidly through the puppy's further training. Problems encountered on the way can hopefully be resolved by a simple phone call or a visit to your professional. However, do not be disheartened if the problem is not with the dog but with yourself, you will not be unique. Certainly do not be too dismayed if your gundog behaves impeccably again when the professional takes control. Remember that those of us with many years in this profession have trained lots of dogs and our reactions are instinctive; being one step ahead comes with practice.

Half-trained

The previous description of part-trained is the only one I would use. However, you will see adverts in the sporting press with part-trained dogs for sale. Beware – these may be genuine, but many are in fact half-trained and come with problems rather than being well schooled, with all the basics firmly instilled and ready to advance to the next level of gundog training.

CONCLUSION

Well done! You have already armed yourself with the first essential piece of dog training equipment, this book, which hopefully will clarify all your training options. Whether you have decided to start with a puppy and carry out all the training personally, seek help from an instructor or trainer, or buy a part-trained or fully trained gundog, it is essential to be prepared with all the necessary equipment and knowledge. In summary, avoid buying expensive gimmicks and seek the advice and services of an expert when help is required.

CHAPTER FIVE

Rearing, Management and Assessment

Rearing and management in the home and/or kennel environment. Socialization. Assessing and developing the puppy's natural, desirable instincts (retrieving and hunting). Subduing or avoiding undesirable behaviour such as barking or chewing. Preparing the puppy for the start of formal training by introduction to noises, smells, lead. Familiarizing the puppy with the wider world.

SOCIALIZATION

Correct, or rather controlled, socialization, beginning immediately the puppy is brought home is of paramount importance to avoid certain behavioural problems from arising. To over-socialize can be as detrimental as under-socialization so a correct balance must be ensured.

Care must be taken when introducing the puppy to other family members, other dogs and particularly children, who should be supervised when with the puppy at all times. The puppy needs to feel confident when it is with you, whatever environment you both happen to be in. However, an over-confident puppy perhaps does not look to its master for guidance and can be very self-willed as the following will illustrate.

The Over-Socialized Pupil

Teaching basic obedience to a client and his seven month old English Springer Spaniel, Jasper, was going fine until I introduced another dog of my own during a lesson, while the client was working with his. Although his dog was quite well advanced with obedience on the lead, this new distraction took the puppy's whole attention away from him. However, after a period of time using close control, discipline was regained until my dog began to hunt the cover in front of Jasper, who was now walking at heel on the lead. Every time I cast mine off to hunt Jasper lunged after it, but was brought to an abrupt halt by the lead. This did not stop him persisting. So every time he lunged and was jerked to a halt he was then turned to be walked away until he had calmed down. Only once he was walking properly at heel and earning praise would he be brought back to try again. It took several attempts before matters improved but then

Correct socialization is of paramount importance and care must be taken when introducing the new puppy to other dogs, friends and family.

he reacted in a different way. When I stopped my dog hunting and left him sitting in front while we discussed progress, Jasper then began lunging while my dog was stationary and the correction as before was repeated.

This young spaniel had been brought up in a city and had been exercised from a little puppy in the local parks, where there was always an abundance of other dogs. He had been allowed to play freely with them and would completely ignore any attempt to stop him playing, so every other strange dog was subsequently seen as a playmate. Not a requirement for the shooting field, or for harmony in public places either.

Meeting and Greeting

This dog was also apparently a nuisance when strangers visited the home, attention seeking all the time and, of course, visitors rewarded him with attention when they arrived and he jumped up. The reaction of most people is to allow a small, appealing, gentle little puppy to jump up and then give it abundant fuss; but six months later they react differently by putting their hands on the now unruly adolescent dog and futilely try to push it down or away. Even if the pushing is accompanied by a raised voice the canine will actually feel rewarded by being touched or shrieked at, and so the behaviour will continue to re-occur in the future.

When one of my small puppies comes up to greet me, I react in the same way as I do with an adult dog. It will only receive fuss if it approaches in the right manner, which should be calmly and with all four feet on the floor. If when I speak to it or touch it gently on the head it then reacts by becoming boisterous the praise is immediately withdrawn

Encouraging a gentle little puppy to jump up for a fuss may cause problems later on.

and the puppy is ignored until it has become calm again. It will soon learn that calmness will gain a pleasurable reward and anything else will be ignored. The puppy has of course already been taught manners by its mother in the nest; she would only allow her puppies to approach and cuddle up or suckle when they did it gently. Any boisterousness or biting would have been swiftly reprimanded with a growl and the milk-bar would have been removed from their reach as the bitch turned her back on them. The subsequent approach by the puppies would then have been much gentler.

Remedial Training

In Jasper's case it is now a matter of making sure that all visitors to the home are made aware of how they should behave when meeting him. Throughout his early life he had been unfortunately conditioned to believe that jumping-up was the required behaviour. If every person who now visits avoids making eye contact, or paying any attention to him physically or orally, but instead every time he approaches in a boisterous manner they fold their arms and turn their back on him, eventually he will calm down and relax. He can then be rewarded for the calm behaviour by his owner, which we wish to now become the norm. Eventually the problem of jumping up will disappear and the new calm behaviour will take its place.

THE PUPPY'S LIVING QUARTERS

I personally believe a youngster is more likely to develop better in a more controlled environment rather than having the absolute freedom of all the rooms in the family home. A purpose-built kennel and run is ideal for the puppy to be confined in when your own attention cannot be fully focused on it, but this kennel must not become a prison cell. At six months old you need a bold pupil ready to start learning to be an obedient companion, not one that may have all sorts of behavioural problems to be dealt with first, such as chewing, barking for attention and coprophagy. Therefore the introduction to its new home must be made as pleasurable as possible. Feed the puppy every mealtime in its own special place, whether a kennel or room in the home, and that will help it to become established as an area of security and comfort. Regular spells of exercise and house-training should take place whether it lives in or out so that good habits are ensured later when taking the dog into vehicles and out in public places.

Chewing

Every puppy will chew to try to alleviate the pain and discomfort of teething at between four and six months of age. A large raw marrow bone will go a long way towards diverting its attentions from damaging articles of importance around the family home or destroying the inside of an expensive wooden kennel. Chewing, however, can become a serious behavioural problem, eventually affecting other aspects of its work if allowed to continue unchecked. It can develop to such a degree that refusal to deliver a dummy or even hard mouth is the sad result later on.

There is really no excuse for allowing a dog to destroy your personal items in the home; if everything was put safely out of reach then the temptation would be removed. Better still, if the dog has its own secure place in the home or purpose-built kennel, with all the chewable edges protected from its teeth by metal, it can be housed safely when your attentions are needed elsewhere.

Be wary also of giving a young puppy your old slippers or other personal items to play with, as it will soon begin to associate items carrying your scent as something that it is allowed to play with, and inevitably destroy items you don't intend it to. Remember that your training dummies, which you will use on a regular basis during later training, will also carry your personal scent, and if a smooth pick-up and delivery is to be achieved then the puppy must not be induced to play alone with such items.

Chewing door frames, furniture, legs of tables, etc. during teething can be stopped by corrective training but as you want your young gundog to eventually work and retrieve enthusiastically for you, then being heavy handed at this age (four to six months) would only damage any trust that it is forming with you and may stop it retrieving altogether. I would advise that if this situation arises the puppy needs to be housed out of temptation's way until it has grown old enough to have been taught basic obedience. I have found with experience that an obedient dog is less likely to misbehave in this way.

Dog Toys

The older dog that has become destructive can be a severe nuisance and tie for its owner, who may be reluctant to leave the animal in the home for even the briefest periods. Many dogs of this nature will probably do most damage immediately the owner leaves, becoming annoyed and frustrated at being left.

You may be able to distract it by using one of the specially designed balls into which part or all of the daily ration of complete feed is inserted. Thus each time you leave the house the ball with its edible contents within will hopefully occupy the dog's mind for the first few vital minutes of isolation. I would not recommend the use of such a toy for the untrained adolescent puppy that is intended to be trained to work in the shooting field, however, as the necessity to scratch and throw the ball about to get the food out could induce subsequent retrieving problems.

Another solution for this type of behaviour that can be easily applied if the dog is housed in a kennel would be to squirt it with water without being seen, using an empty washing-up liquid bottle or hose-pipe, every time the dog became agitated at being left. This may be all that is required to persuade it to retreat to the sleeping box to wait calmly for your return and subsequent reward. You must be vigilant and have great patience to begin with, but persevere and the required response will be achieved. As with any dog training matter, avoiding the problem developing by using common sense, in particular by removing boredom from the puppy's life, is much easier than effecting a cure for a seriously ingrained behavioural problem later on.

ASSESSING AND DEVELOPING NATURAL RETRIEVING INSTINCTS

All retriever, spaniel and HPR puppies of true working strain are born with the desire to pick up and carry any item that arouses

Play with a tennis ball to assess the puppy's natural retrieving instinct.

Training lanes will help with return and delivery.

their interest. It is therefore up to me as the trainer to nurture and develop this desire in the youngster and encourage it to bring these items back to me right from the start. Common sense and patience are essential if I am to achieve the correct response.

Precious Items

Very often the first thing that a puppy picks up when introduced to the family home will be an item very delicate or precious to some member of the household. If your instinctual response is to panic and raise your voice then the puppy's response will be either to spit it out instantly or to run away and keep well out of harm's way.

Whatever the item is, you should remain calm, speaking softly and endearingly to encourage the puppy to come to you. If it is still reluctant then sit on the floor and just wait patiently until curiosity gets the better of the puppy, when hopefully it will join you in a flurry of licks and furiously wagging tail. If at this point the puppy still holds the prize in its mouth then pick it up and give it lots of fuss before gently easing the object from its grip. To nurture trust, immediately replace the object with one that the puppy is allowed, such as its favourite canine toy, ball or knuckle bone.

Play Retrieves

During the puppy's early months I always carry a tennis ball in my jacket pocket, so that on the puppy's frequent short walks I can occasionally play with it and further assess its instinct to retrieve. I am always wary of the surroundings when first attempting this, as any distractions will severely hamper the puppy's attention on me. I avoid dropping the ball where game or other scents are likely to be in abundance. I try at all times during these early lessons to keep the ball away from nettles or prickly or thick undergrowth, and in view of the puppy as it bobbles along the ground.

My puppy is allowed to run in every time until I am certain that it is so keen to fetch the ball that momentary restraint will not deter it when released again. At this point in time I gently pick up the puppy before rolling the ball away in full view. Then I release the puppy quickly to allow it to chase after the moving object. Hopefully it will pick up and bring back the ball to me, and I make sure that lots of fuss is given before I take the ball gently from the puppy's mouth.

Boredom

There is always a danger that the consistent natural retriever can be bored into becoming unreliable by constant repetition of this fun exercise. One or two play retrieves a day is more than adequate if we are going to intensify rather than inhibit this natural behaviour. If I have a puppy that under no circumstances will bring the ball to me but instead runs and hides or, as quite often happens especially with Cocker puppies, it decides to bury it then, as I have no control yet, common sense must prevail.

There are two courses of action I may take, depending on the age of the puppy; if it is six months or older now is the time to begin the obedience training and I will leave any further retrieving alone until the puppy has been taught to return to me on my recall command. To persist in trying to recall a puppy to you or give other commands which it cannot understand only instils disobedience and causes you to lose confidence and maybe become impatient.

Training Lanes

If the puppy is younger than six months, then matters can very often be improved by ingenuity. I have several narrow training lanes, both natural and man-made, where I can tempt a reluctant deliverer to return to me, and every time it does so the puppy receives lots of gentle praise, hopefully until the penny drops and a strong urge to return to me develops. A path edged by heavy undergrowth is a useful natural channel for a puppy to return along. Be prepared to sit or even lie on the ground so that it can come right in to your body. I try to divert my eyes from the puppy's as it returns to me, so avoiding a threatening stare which may cause hesitation, and I never grab or snatch the ball from the mouth, but pick the pup up and give it fuss first. In fact, if improvement is to be made, I must try not to touch the ball at all until the puppy is ready to release it of its own accord.

With care the puppy's natural instincts can be reliably developed before formal training begins. Unfortunately, however, many of my clients' older trainees come with retrieving problems, which means it is likely that this trial and error type of play training was not used correctly.

DEVELOPING A PUPPY'S NATURAL HUNTING INSTINCTS

Throughout a young puppy's growing and development period, before formal training begins at around six months of age, I try to bring out as much of its natural hunting ability as possible.

It is pointless just leaving the youngster confined in a kennel where it will learn nothing and its senses, such as smell, will be dulled, rather than made keener by the frequent exposure to game scent, which I like to give them. No matter what the breed, as soon as my puppies are protected by the necessary course of vaccinations I begin taking them over the fields where they can come into contact with the world outside the usual kennel or home environment.

Rabbit Droppings

Each puppy may react differently to the strange objects, smells and noises it will encounter on these early walks, and at all times

Steadiness to tame tumbler pigeons achieved.

I immediately give verbal encouragement if my young charge shows any signs of being afraid. I will allow it to investigate thoroughly any scent that is found; rabbit droppings may disappear down the gullet quickly, but if the puppy is wormed regularly it will come to no harm, and it would be detrimental to the bond building process if I were to constantly chastise it to try to stop this.

Introducing Cover

I take care to avoid upsetting the learning process by the puppy becoming irritated by thistles, nettles or other such harmful undergrowth; after all, I want to develop a strong desire for this future gundog, especially if a spaniel, to enter cover freely. Rabbit or other game scent may often draw the puppy into cover, and if luck is on my side the puppy may even bump into the real thing. It soon will become intent on achieving this objective each time the same spot or scent is encountered. If a chase does ensue then I just wait for the puppy's return, whereupon it will receive lots of praise and fuss. I am not therefore giving reward for the chase, but for coming back willingly to me. This is not the right time in its development to start insisting on steadiness.

Using Treats

The puppy that is slower to develop the urge to investigate cover naturally can be encouraged by the use of strategically placed titbits in a familiar patch of light undergrowth. I break small pieces of a pressed hide chew or some other treat and drop them into the cover in view of the puppy, who will eventually overcome its fear of entering the undergrowth to investigate the delicious aroma. Be patient, for once the puppy has succeeded in finding a tasty morsel and as its enthusiasm increases when searching for a reward, you can gradually increase the difficulty incurred by using thicker cover and smaller titbits. Throughout this early development period I use verbal encouragement when the dog is entering the cover or is close to finding a reward.

Search Commands

At this stage you are not trying to start the dog hunting, but instead indicating it is in the right area to find the treat. I use the word 'There' to indicate when it is getting close to its objective. 'Hi lost' is also a common phrase used by some trainers for this purpose. However, it does not really matter what command is used as long as you are consistent. The puppy will begin to learn by your repetition of the same chosen search command, and it is useful to get them accustomed to the term now during play training.

Self-Taught Steadiness to Birds

I am fortunate to have some tame tumbler pigeons in the rabbit pen; these will conveniently drop onto the ground foraging for food in front of the puppy, whose first reaction will normally be to rush at them. The pigeons will just flutter up to the shed roof out of harm's way each time this happens and then drop back down when the puppy has been moved away. Without any interference from me, the puppy will soon realize that to pursue the birds once they have taken to the air is futile, and after several attempts to catch one will begin to exercise self-restraint. Then each time they lift the pup will stop and watch them, before dropping its head to sniff and investigate the scent on the ground where they have been feeding.

The same logic can be applied in the autumn when the swallows are gathering ready to migrate. At this time they will fly low over the stubbles, searching for flying insects to build up their fat reserves for the long trip ahead. To a keen young dog that has not yet learned to exercise self-control, a chase may, indeed will, be irresistible. However, there is no chance of succeeding in catching or even getting close to one of these fast little birds and this lack of success each time gradually decreases the length of the chase. Without human intervention the youngster soon loses interest.

Barking

I am able, throughout these early adventures, to assess the puppy in other departments. The occasional puppy which shows enthusiasm by whining or barking during these assessments will be carefully monitored during early formal training so that the fault can be subdued sufficiently to still enable its use as a serious prospect for the field later on.

The Forward Puppy

Sometimes a puppy may be extremely bold and apparently fearless, surmounting every problem it encounters naturally with ease. Be very careful not to advance this type of puppy too quickly through its training, as bad habits will be learned just as quickly. Small mistakes or omissions early on can take a lot of skill, time and effort to put right.

PREP SCHOOL

Having previously assessed and developed the young puppy's natural retrieving and hunting instincts I now like to spend a week or two introducing it to as many new situations as possible in preparation for the start of the formal schooling at around seven months old.

To take an untrained, unsocialized gundog puppy that does not know me from its kennel at seven months old, put a lead straight on and expect an immediate willing response to obedience training would of course be asking the impossible. At the very least one could expect the puppy to become very agitated, and maybe even frightened. At most I could only expect a reluctant compliance with my wishes. Worse still, aggression responses such as fear biting could be induced.

Most gundog puppies of good working strain have an inbuilt desire to try to please their master if allowed the opportunity to start to develop the necessary mutual trust. I have already begun this process in the initial assessment period and hopefully a bond is already being nurtured. Whatever happens now I must not upset this growing respect by heavy handling.

Introducing the Collar

For the puppy's first introduction to the collar I bide my time, waiting until it is in a very playful mood, and then I gently slip a light collar over its head and allow it immediate freedom to run and play as before. If panic is the immediate reaction, I pick the puppy up if still small enough and try to distract it with lots of fuss. When sufficiently distracted from the cause of its previous anxiety and its muscles relax, I once again put the puppy down and encourage free play. If concern is shown again, I will keep repeating this reassurance until the collar around its neck has been accepted. As soon as a little progress has been made I remove the collar and put it back into my pocket ready for use another time.

I will not repeat this lesson too often, but gradually over several days the collar will be accepted and so ignored whilst play continues with it still in place around the neck. When this point has been reached I will substitute the collar with a heavy link slip chain of the correct length to suit the puppy's neck size

'I am not sure I can do this...'

and repeat the process as before until that no longer bothers it either.

The Lead

I can now attach a lead to the collar, which is just left to trail behind it. If necessary, I repeat the same procedure as for the collar until the puppy is again relaxed and happy to wear it.

This is now the time when I begin to show my puppy that, although it may feel restraint through the lead, if it complies with my wishes then it will be rewarded. Picking up the end of the lead I verbally cajole and encourage the pup to follow me; you can be as silly as you like here to get the pup to approach or follow to receive some fuss. If cajoling and animated body language fails to impress refrain from jerking the lead but just keep a little pressure on it until it has the desired effect.

Patience is a must at this stage; I want the puppy to be reassured and happy when it is coming to me or walking calmly by my side. The pup should quickly begin to learn that bouncing away will be met with firm, quiet restraint, whereas it can fully expect to feel the pleasure from the gentle stroke of my hand and soft verbal encouragement when it comes close to me. I am not at this stage trying to teach it to walk to heel, only to overcome any possible fear of the restraint of the lead.

Restraint at Mealtime

The seeds of compliance to discipline can also be sown at meal times. During early puppyhood the youngster has been allowed to dive straight in to the food bowl as soon as it was placed on the floor. I begin teaching restraint gradually over a few days, starting with holding the puppy firmly in my arms before putting the bowl down.

Most puppies, especially those from large litters, have been conditioned to dive in quickly for fear of there being nothing left in the bowl to eat. This will definitely mean the puppy will struggle to be released as it sees the food bowl being placed on the floor. I do not give in to these futile struggles but wait until calmness is apparent and then I release my hold. Each mealtime I take the lesson a small step further, first restraining the pup in a sitting position, then slowly releasing my

'...Yes I can, mum's over there and I'm hungry!'

grip whilst keeping the pup sitting. My hands are in a position close to the puppy so that I can immediately deliver restraint again if it makes any attempt to move.

As each of these stages is reinforced with food, the learning process develops quite quickly until eventually the pup will stand or sit and wait as I put the bowl down without any physical intervention from me. Now any attempt to dive in before the order to eat is given will be greeted with the bowl swiftly being lifted away so that reward is not gained for the incorrect behaviour. My eventual aim is for the dog to instantly stop and wait for my command to eat when the food is put in front of it without any verbal instruction from me. Is this the beginning of steadiness? It is indeed sowing the seeds of obedience and control.

WORLDLY WISE

I want the puppy to trust me as its safe guardian. The more the puppy is aware of and used to by the time formal training begins at six or seven months of age, the better. I want, then, to give myself every chance to be the centre of the puppy's attention during each lesson, which is impossible if the puppy is afraid of its environment, every little noise, strange object, beast or movement.

Livestock

I introduce the puppy carefully to any livestock encountered on our outings; this is where the lead is very important. Most youngsters become very concerned when they come face to face with horses or cattle for the first time and the fearful, panic response may be to try to bolt for cover, sometimes with the livestock in hot pursuit, which will only heighten the puppy's fears that they are under attack. With the security of the lead attached I have the control to be able to restrain this fear reaction and offer reassurance or guidance.

The very bold puppy may have already learned the enjoyment of chasing a rabbit or two, and perhaps will now eye sheep as a larger alternative. Here again the lead is necessary to prevent an uncontrollable situation arising. Once obedience and mutual

Early training will give an older dog more confidence when travelling later on in life, Purdey shows no hesitation in getting in the trailer used on shoot days.

trust has been developed during the subsequent formal training, then and only then, can the lead be dispensed with in these testing circumstances.

Travelling

I introduce the puppy to the car, travelling box or dog trailer at an early age. So many dogs do not travel well in later life as the only times they were taken out as youngsters ended up first with isolation from their siblings, to be taken to an unfamiliar place (your home), and then the second outing ended with an unpleasant experience at the local vet's. It may be necessary, indeed very sensible, to accustom the puppy to living in a travelling box in the home or kennel first so that it becomes the place of security and of course very familiar in looks and smell.

Even with this familiarity the puppy may be unduly worried at entering the car, and if gentle persuasion does not work then I resort to tasty morsels each time I put the puppy in. Although not a great believer in treats as a means of teaching obedience, they do certainly work in this situation. The previous hesitation should soon be forgotten and confidence at jumping in will soon result. However, small puppies will be unable to jump in and out of large cars or 4×4s, and it is sensible to avoid possible injury by continuing to lift them in and out until they are mature enough to withstand the jump. The alternative is to provide a ramp so that they can clamber in unaided to find their treat.

Jumping

I find that teaching a puppy to jump confidently on command over gradually increasing heights before attempting to get it to jump into the car removes many of the difficulties that are commonly encountered. But that will happen much later in the pup's development. However, the confidence to get over something begins with the puppies that I breed as soon they are old enough to clamber out of the whelping box. The incentive is again a food reward, either toddling after mum for a drink or, when weaning, a more urgent scrabble to the bowl full of tasty food in competition with their siblings. I can gently extend the difficulty factor by adding more boards across the doorway to their kennel, which they must get over each time to feed. As the puppies grow so the height of the barrier is increased a few inches at a time. This same logic can be applied for the puppy in the family home, but be careful that the boards are not left in place across doorways when friends come to visit.

Noise Reaction

The modern strains of working gundog have been selectively bred over a period of time to produce a kind, biddable animal which is relatively easy for the novice to handle and train. This can mean that some individuals have an underlying sensitivity and, if not treated with common sense when introducing gunfire, could exhibit some degree of nervousness to the gun.

I use systematic desensitization to avoid this problem, and so begin to introduce noises gradually throughout the puppy's infancy. Metal bowls make quite a clatter when dropped on the floor, but as they are associated with something pleasant any surprise is soon forgotten – the sound of them being filled will come to be identified as a prelude to feeding. Using this same principle of the puppy's attention being strongly focused on something it desires, I am able to introduce gradually different types of noise whilst the puppy is distracted – for example, during exercise when it is investigating fresh scent that it has found, or perhaps when it is playing with the other dogs. Later on the draw of rabbits in the pen or watching a dummy in the air will be also used to create a diversion from the offending sound.

Clay Shoots

As confidence grows I keep exposing the puppy further. A visit to the local clay shoot may be a good idea, but take matters cautiously. I will stop the car some distance from the action to monitor the initial response to the noise and will take it closer only if there is no sign of an adverse reaction. Little and often is the keynote to lasting success – any dog showing fear at this stage will not benefit from being progressed too quickly.

Fear of the Weapon

Although the puppy may have been desensitized to the noise, or indeed it may never have shown any signs of fear on hearing a loud report, I have come across a few individuals who showed varying degrees of concern the first time I carried the actual weapon. This is easily prevented with common sense at an early age, as familiarity with any object will prevent the problem arising. So right from the start I carry a gun or a long walking stick under my arm during feeding and exercise until the puppy shows no sign of apprehension at its presence.

Water

I try to avoid introducing the puppy to water too soon. I do not want the first contact to be a frightening experience, which very often happens if the youngster is following the example of the older dogs when it may jump straight in out of its depth and come up coughing up both weed and water. For the smaller breeds exercising out on rainy days can produce big enough puddles to enable a smoother introduction. But of course I do not force the issue. If your particular puppy has no intention of taking the plunge a full introduction to water can be left until later, when training is well under way and the puppy has matured both physically and mentally.

CONCLUSION

The puppy needs to enjoy this early part of its development. However, the more it is aware of, and used to, when formal training begins the better. At that time I want to be the centre of its attention each lesson, which is impossible if it is unhappy or withdrawn and afraid of every object, noise, movement or smell.

CHAPTER SIX

Formal Training: The Keystone for Future Success

The age to start and the methods used to teach basic obedience, heelwork, sit and stay, recall, etc. Increasing control and getting the puppy focused. Steadiness to moving objects and game. Extending the dog's range of commands (vocabulary), including verbal, whistle and visual signals.

WHAT AGE TO START

When the puppy's physical and mental development is well advanced, usually at around six or seven months of age, it is time to begin the serious business of turning an adolescent from a potential reprobate into a pleasant, obedient lifelong friend and family companion. This is only a guide; it is possible to teach basic obedience to older dogs too, and I have had success with two- and three-year-olds.

CHANGE OF ROUTINE

During this early formal training period the puppy's routine management will change and its freedom in the outside world should be temporarily curtailed so that the serious formal obedience training process can begin in a very controlled environment, free from distractions.

Kennelled Dogs

A kennelled dog's exercise will now be socializing and playing with the other kennel occupants twice a day in the kennel yard until this part of its training is advanced to the point that control off the lead can be maintained, when once again it will be taken out into the wide open spaces of the countryside.

Family Dogs

It is sometimes difficult to convince all the members of the household that the puppy reared in the family home will come to no harm if its free exercise or long walks on the lead are stopped for a few weeks. Family members can keep the puppy stimulated with sensible playtime in the garden. Everyone should understand that basic obedience training needs to be consistent. It is no use walking the puppy in a casual way on the lead when out for a walk, and then expecting it to focus on you when using the lead to teach heelwork.

Thomas (the author's grandson) with his lifelong friend and obedient companion Archie.

EARLY LESSONS

Frequency and Length of Lessons

A young or untrained dog's concentration span can be quite limited. The length of the training session will depend on the individual trainee; however, I find a fifteen minute lesson, once or twice a day, to be sufficient to make good progress during early discipline training.

Expected Progress

By the end of a six to eight week period, using this suggested frequency and length of lesson, I would expect my young pupil to walk on my left side 'at heel' on and off the lead, sit on command to voice, whistle, visual hand signal, or even a clap of the hands if a spaniel, stay on the drop while I walk away and around it, and come to me when called, whilst at all times maintaining good eye contact. In other words, it will be attentive and obedient to my wishes while working in an environment free of distractions. It will also have developed a good degree of self-control and have begun to react properly to certain situations before being asked.

Vocabulary

The vocabulary of voice and whistle commands that the young dog responds to will also be gradually increasing, but I consciously keep this list as short as is practicable. It should be acknowledging its own name, the word 'No' and the following firm commands, for which a definite action will be required by the puppy:

- 'Heel', to follow by my side;
- 'Sit', to put its bottom firmly on the ground;

- 'Stay', to wait motionless until I give another command;
- 'Here', to return to me;
- 'Kennel', to enter the kennel or go away from me through any door, gate or opening such as the house or car.

As previously highlighted, the novice trainer is advised to spend some time deciding what commands they are going to use and thinking about how to condition their puppy to respond to each with the correct action, before embarking on this stage of the training. Good preparation – learning the theory first and establishing firmly in your own mind how you will proceed – will help you to avoid possible confusion induced by a change of command midway through training.

Body language and, in particular, the hands also play an important role in training and handling. I try at all times to catch the puppy's eye by subtle movements or clear hand signals to obtain a favourable response which can then be positively reinforced.

BASIC OBEDIENCE

I shall now guide you through this essential basic obedience course from the beginning, in some detail.

The first important rule to remember if you want to instil obedience is that you must never give a command that you are unable to enforce immediate compliance with. Second, remain calm and collected at all times and never lose your temper. If matters seem to be deteriorating, put the puppy away until you have thought the situation through over a cup of tea or have sought the advice of an experienced trainer. There is always a logical solution to any problem, no matter how big it seems to the first-time trainer.

Conditioning the Dog's Attention

Throughout the early rearing it has been possible for me to nurture the puppy's desire to be with me using positive reinforcement, so that its attention on me has developed to the stage where it is actually looking to me for guidance, reassurance, food or praise on a regular basis. This enables me to teach the pup any new skills more easily. However, most people who seek my advice have not been able to get their dog focused on them at all. It really is quite easy to develop this, but it is also easy to get it wrong, and stop the youngster focusing on you by incorrect actions during early rearing. For instance, when teaching a small puppy to sit before it eats its food some owners unwittingly teach it to look at the bowl before eating, instead of looking at them for the visual instruction to eat.

Common Sense

It is common sense that if you want a behaviour to reoccur then it must be rewarded, and if you want it to diminish or be extinguished then it is not rewarded, or is punished. It is all too easy to get in the habit of using the pup's name in a loud voice as a telling off when it does something wrong; so why would it then want to look at you when you use its name in this formal training? The name has gradually become conditioned as a punisher. If, however, the puppy heard its name always delivered in a friendly tone, and subsequently was rewarded with praise or a treat every time, by the time formal training started it would be looking at you eagerly every time you say its name. It is never too late to correct your previous actions – it may just take a little time and patience.

Heelwork

The puppy has already learned the simple meaning of 'Sit' and 'Stay' at mealtimes during prep school, so I can now begin the basic obedience training by teaching the youngster to follow me wherever I go. This is the key to the success of all the following lessons. If the puppy really has an urge to be with me, it will also be watching me attentively and this will make the learning process so much smoother. Forcing a puppy to do things will not develop trust, and its master will be viewed with suspicion and, worse still, sometimes with fear.

A correctly fitted slip chain, with slack leather lead.

I have already accustomed (desensitized) the puppy to wearing something around its neck such as a collar or choke chain and lead during prep school, so that it does not cause irritation or concern now. It is just a matter of insisting that on my command of 'Heel', coupled with slapping my hand on my thigh, it follows quietly without pulling or sniffing the ground and regulates its pace automatically with mine. It sounds simple enough, but in reality this task is completely alien to some of the different breeds' natural instincts. A retriever breed usually is the easiest but there are always exceptions. One of the hard-hunting spaniel or HPR breeds who has already enjoyed the freedom of the outside world will instinctively want to be away hunting and enjoying itself, and not confined by discipline. Whatever the breed, it is up to me to condition the puppy using positive reinforcement so that following quietly by my side at heel is a mutual pleasure for the pup and I. There are going to be many times in the future when you will need this close control when out in public places.

Choice of Lead

For these heelwork lessons I tend to use a large oval link choke or slip chain of the correct length to suit the particular dog; as a guide, use a 20in (50cm) chain for a small Cocker bitch, up to 30in (75cm) for a Labrador dog, attached to a soft lead of rope or leather that is about 4ft 6in (1.4m) in length. I have

Taking one step forward with my right leg, and holding the dog in the stay position with hand signal and verbal 'Stay' command.

My left hand leads the dog to my side as I move the left leg forward with the verbal command 'Heel'.

I give the dog immediate praise for doing right.

found small link or curb chains to be too severe and more likely to cause discomfort, and if a shorter lead is used there may be a tendency for pressure to be applied unnecessarily. However, some puppies are so easy and gentle that an ordinary rope or soft leather slip lead will give the same excellent results and they are certainly very convenient to slip in the jacket pocket to use for all adult dogs later on, once this basic skill has been thoroughly learned. I prefer not to use a fixed collar as any pressure applied to the lead is directed fully to the front of the throat, whereas a slip lead spreads the pressure around the neck.

I form the chain into a slip collar and attach the free end to the lead; the chain is then placed over the puppy's head and around its neck, with the free end, lead attached, hanging loosely underneath its chin.

The Positive Method

I begin this lesson to 'follow me' with the pup now sitting nice and still on my left-hand side. Any fidgeting or attempts to change position are not allowed. I move very slowly at first; I take one step forward with my right leg only and make sure the pup does not move by giving the stay command with voice and associated hand signal of the open palm pushed towards the pup's face. I reward the 'Sit' and the 'Stay' as they occur with verbal praise and do not allow any subsequent movement. If when I say 'Good dog' the pup does begin to move then a little check on the lead coupled with a verbal punisher, 'Aagh', is delivered immediately so that the movement is less likely to reoccur next time.

If all goes well I am now in the position of having my right leg one step out in front, with my left hand stretched back with the open palm towards the dog, whose eyes should be focused on it. I can now use this hand to lead the dog to come to my side as I simultaneously move my left leg to join my right, slap my left thigh and say 'Heel'. The pup should move forward, following the left hand as it moves away from its eyes towards my leg, and come to my left leg while still looking at the left hand which has led it there. I give immediate praise by stroking it with the hand for this simple movement. I do not let it go past but make it sit at my side again, before repeating the process.

This is like dancing lessons, learning one step at a time before being allowed to move freely across the floor. You want the dog's focus on you and it must want to learn willingly, not be reluctantly obedient through the use of negative methods. Once this first step has been mastered the pup should move to your side and stop of its own accord. Only then should you progress and, as it comes to a stop, move the right leg forward another step and subsequently the left, but make sure the pup now stops again to receive your praise as before.

Not only is the dog being conditioned to follow your left hand and leg at heel, but the seeds of recall are also being sown through these 'follow me' lessons.

The Negative Method

This method has been used for decades but, whilst the result can be the same as previously described, this method can also result in an unhappy-looking dog, tail down, walking reluctantly at your side if the positive reinforcement for the correct behaviour is not properly conducted.

With the end of the lead held loosely in the right hand, you begin walking and give the 'Heel' voice and visual commands to allow the puppy also to move. Each time the puppy pulls ahead, stop walking and check it with a swift jerk of the lead using the left hand. Immediately let the lead go slack again, which in turn releases the tension of the chain or lead around the dog's neck. The same logic is applied if the puppy does not follow; it is given a jerk on the lead to force it to move forward. If the chain remains tight when the pressure is taken off the lead then check to make sure it is on the puppy's neck the correct way round. Reiterating the 'heel' command, again move slowly forward, being ready to stop and respond by a jerk with the left hand each time the puppy misbehaves. Every time the puppy is in the correct position and walking nicely on a slack lead, with its attention focused on you, give plenty of verbal praise to reinforce this desired behaviour.

This last sentence is the most important part of this method and something that many forget – good behaviour must be rewarded, otherwise the dog will never learn to do the right thing willingly.

Slow Progress

With either method progress may be very slow for the first week or two but do not worry for your patience will eventually be repaid. I make absolutely sure that each time success is achieved I continue to reward the pupil with a kind voice and a gentle stroke with the hand; after all, it must learn when it is doing right, if I am to gain respect and build confidence. A young puppy's attention span is very limited, so a ten to fifteen minute lesson once or twice a day is adequate at this stage. The lesson begins and ends happily at the kennel door or at its special place of security in the home.

As the puppy is already sure of the familiar training environment being used, it makes it much easier to retain its complete attention throughout the lesson. Once success has been achieved in these familiar surroundings, only then can the lessons be extended to include new areas and different surfaces underfoot. The difference in behaviour when you take a puppy, which is very proficient at walking on the lead on a concrete path, onto a new surface such as tarmac, gravel or grass can be amazing. The change of surface underfoot can cause a change in attitude, and so the conditioning process has to be repeated in each new environment.

The Sit

Once the puppy is beginning to follow quite willingly and, more importantly, with its full attention focused on me, I can now go on to the command 'Sit'. For my own canine trainees I now always use 'Sit' coupled with a raised open hand signal given simultaneously. Although I have previously taught this command during early rearing and prep school when the puppy was required to sit and wait at feed times, I now want it to respond obediently to the command each time I give it in this new and every subsequent situation. Because the lead is attached I can insist on compliance with the command every time, by using a tug on the lead to enforce the action of sitting and by physically manipulating the dog into position if it is necessary. Having been conditioned to sit on the same command for food over several weeks prior, immediate compliance under ideal training conditions is not usually a problem at this stage.

Expected Progress

After two or three weeks' patient but firm work with the choke chain or slip lead I would ideally expect my pupil to maintain eye contact and react automatically to my changing body movements, regulating pace and direction with mine, without me having to remind it too often with a command or a correction with the lead. The success of later training will all hinge on how well the puppy is taught these early lessons. Achieving less than strict compliance at this stage could have serious repercussions in the future, with a gradual breakdown of obedience.

Eye Contact

A common problem that often occurs is a lapse of attention once obedience training has begun. This is clearly apparent when, although the puppy is walking quietly by the trainer's side, its eyes are looking everywhere except at its 'master'. This obvious lapse of concentration must be rectified before it develops into a real issue. Each time its attention wanders use a little tug on the lead to remind it you are still there, and when it subsequently turns its head to look at you, give gentle praise and enough fuss to show that you are pleased with its renewed attention. Make these obedience lessons very brief, away from all distractions, until progress is eventually made and the puppy's attention is again focused on you.

Working Off Lead

When the puppy is at the stage where the lead, although attached, is never being used for correction only then will I advance to this next important stage. In a confined area or narrow training corridor or lane I can now test its reactions when the lead is detached from the chain, or the slip lead is allowed to trail or, better still, is loosely coiled round its neck to keep it off the floor. I will use all the same body language and commands as before but will be alert and ready to stop the dog if it shows any desire to break from my side – if necessary by grabbing the chain, then reconnecting the lead, and continuing as before until I am confident that we are both settled and ready to try off lead again.

Sensitive Puppy

Sometimes a very sensitive puppy may be reluctant to follow when the lead is detached and the chain left around its neck. Verbal cajoling may be all that is necessary to have the desired effect and make it move towards and follow you, but do not let this become an issue. It is often better to reconnect the lead and take control. Be careful; even if complete success is quickly achieved and control at heel off lead seems fine, be in no rush to dispense with the chain or slip lead completely yet, as the extra security and direct control it affords will be beneficial during further formal training.

Normal Puppy

Most puppies will walk a few steps perfectly well off lead at first. If so, praise is immediately given and the lead is re-attached. I build up the distance walked minus lead very slowly over time. It is extremely important that a puppy does not get away from the trainer's side at all, so you must be fully focused on the task and your dog's reactions. Once I am sure we are together I will remove the lead and chain completely and repeat the previous gradual steps cautiously, as with nothing around the pup's neck the strong-willed pupil may just try to break away. However, if the previous stages have been carefully worked through this should not be an issue.

Strong-Willed Puppy

The occasional strong-willed puppy can be quite a challenge to control off lead, and great care must be used to make sure it cannot get away from the handler and show even more disobedience by keeping out of reach. It may just be that it has been allowed to run free in the park with other dogs every time the lead was removed as a puppy, so now the removal has been conditioned as a cue to go and play. With this type of problem I would attach a second, very light lead, and then as the chain is removed I would still have the power to stop the pup when it first tries to break away. Until I have taught perfect compliance in very confined areas I would never risk taking this type of puppy out into the open at this stage.

Stay

Once the puppy is sitting consistently on voice command and/or hand signal, I will then extend the use of the verbal command 'Stay', which is coupled with the visual signal of the open raised hand thrust towards the pupil to deter it from following me as I slowly back away a couple of paces to the end of the lead. If the pup moves I put it back on the exact spot where it was seated originally. A tip to make sure that it is the exact spot the puppy left is to mark the ground with the heel of your foot before beginning the lesson, then you can be sure that exact compliance can be achieved should the puppy move.

When success is apparent and the pup has remained motionless for a few seconds, I then return to it and reward the behaviour with a gentle stroke under the chin. If this causes the puppy to become too excited and subsequently begin to stand or move, I immediately remove my hand and, with a scolding 'No' or 'Aagh', put it back immediately into a sitting position. It will soon learn that if it remains calm and still, the pleasure of gentle affection will always follow, so the desired behaviour is

Any attempt to move from the stay must be stopped immediately.

being conditioned through the use of positive reinforcement.

I gradually increase the distance I back away, dropping the still-attached lead on the ground once the end is reached, and also gradually increase the length of time that the puppy is left on the drop. It is as well to keep an eye on your watch and set yourself targets to reach. Start with fifteen seconds and gradually build up over a week or two to three or four minutes. Do not try to achieve too much too quickly, but instead aim to make progress slowly over the weeks. Every successful increase in distance and time will help speed progress, but if you stretch things to the point of failure then I am afraid that progress will be not be smooth or consistent.

The Recall

There is a temptation to introduce the recall now, but although I want to heighten the desire for the puppy to come to me I never call the puppy up to me from this seated position when teaching the stay command. I am teaching the puppy to allow me to move away from it while it remains perfectly still; to do the opposite and call the pup off the drop would only induce the puppy to wrongly anticipate my wishes, causing confusion and unsteadiness.

Off Lead

I now further test the puppy by removing the lead completely and repeating the lesson already learned. I then try walking round it in a circle. Again it may attempt to move or follow. But compliance is insisted on and I put it back on the spot each time it moves, not physically by lifting it, but by pointing to the spot and getting it to go back there of its own accord. This helps build my authority as the 'pack leader'. Patience and perseverance will eventually pay off over a period of time, and each success can be steadily built on until the puppy is reliably and attentively waiting for my return while I turn my back to walk away or move briefly out of sight. Rewarded by voice at a distance helps confirm that it is doing right.

As with the early 'heelwork' lessons I removed distraction by using a familiar place each time and up to this point I have used the same spot for each 'stay' lesson. I now begin to vary the locations used, always walking the pup 'at heel' to and from the spot, from the kennel or car, so that I am always well in control of the situation. Remember, make sure that no matter how well or badly the lesson has gone you must always part as friends at the kennel door, offering the pup praise, a pat and perhaps a biscuit.

Recall

I do not feel the need to teach the recall in the conventional way by making the puppy sit while I walk away and then call it in to me. That is another trial and error method, and is not always successful because the temptation is to try to attempt this long before the puppy has been made fully obedient. Should disobedience occur, perhaps even in a slight way by reluctance to come quickly or sniffing the ground on the way, the trainer is powerless to enforce immediate compliance because of the distance separating them and the pupil. The temptation may then be to raise the voice, which would only confirm to the pupil that it should remain where it is or, worse still, run away.

Throughout the heelwork, sit and stay lessons the puppy has been kept under full control and has received ample reward for being close to me. It therefore has a very strong urge to be close to me whenever possible. Therefore the recall will now be a very natural extension of the obedience training; the only additional things that the dog will need to be taught are the whistle, verbal and visual commands associated with it.

Verbal and Visual Recall Commands

My verbal command 'Here' sounds very like 'Heel' for good reason, and therefore is easily introduced. I have never previously called the puppy from the stay position but I will now do this in a particular situation – going through a gate. Previously when walking through a gate I have sat the pup, opened the gate, told it to 'Stay' as I have moved through one pace then called it to walk through at heel in the same way that I have taught it to follow me in the open. Now I will change the procedure at the gate and, instead of calling it to 'Heel', I will face the pup and encourage it with the command 'Here' delivered in a friendly tone. I simultaneously drop my hand low in a welcoming gesture to get the pup to come straight towards me and sit to receive praise. Due to the similarity of verbal command and body language in the familiar environment of the gate then this is almost certainly going to work first time, but I would encourage you to use a long, slack lead just in case compliance needs enforcing. For some weeks this will be the only situation when I will give the puppy the 'Stay' command and then subsequently

The recall using 'Here' and a welcoming hand signal to come towards me from the sitting position.

Alan Munns teaching Jasper steadiness to thrown dummies.

call it up from a distance using 'Here' (albeit only a short distance at this time).

Incidentally, if the puppy begins to pre-empt the recall through the gate then shutting the gate in its face will soon deter it from trying. This of course applies when my dogs are loose in the exercise run; they are only allowed to come out individually when the gate is opened and when they hear their name, otherwise their path is blocked by the gate. These good manners are insisted upon when leaving the car, kennel or house.

STEADINESS

During early puppyhood, before formal training began, my young gundog puppy was allowed to run free and inevitably it had the opportunity to chase the odd bird or rabbit it encountered on the many outings into the open countryside. At that time the puppy was not doing anything wrong by chasing, just following one of its natural inherited instincts. I now need to control that predatory desire if the young pupil is going to become a reliable, steady shooting companion for the rest of its working life. Indeed, any responsible owner should teach their dog not to chase, whether they are a working gundog or the family pet.

To some shooting people, the meaning of a 'steady dog', although being well under control, is a slow potterer who exhibits very little drive or enthusiasm in its work. This latter description is definitely not what I want to achieve when teaching steadiness. I want the dog to retain its enthusiasm, eagerness and speed. If it is a hunting breed then it needs drive when hunting, as well as being trustworthy and steady when game is found, flushed or shot. Close control, walking at heel,

Alan keeps his attention on Jasper while he collects all the dummies by hand.

sitting, staying and coming to the handler on command have been well instilled over the past few weeks so we are now going to introduce a degree of self-control and steadiness.

Steady to Thrown Dummies

Steadiness is not taught in one particular way; every situation that could cause a dog to run after something that is moving must be dealt with separately. First I would want to stop the dog moving from the seated position, and praise must be given to enforce this lack of movement. With the dog in the stay position throw dummies carefully around so that any attempt to move can be intercepted immediately by putting yourself physically in between the dog and the dummy.

Your dog should never be rewarded by being allowed to retrieve any of the dummies thrown in this way. Always pick them up yourself, but keep your attention focused on your dog as you do so. It must not move, but should remain firmly seated until you return to its side to give praise. Over time the dummies thrown in this frequently repeated exercise will no longer hold a strong attraction for the dog.

Sitting to Flush

To achieve full self-control to a flush I will sow the seeds of steadiness to movement gradually throughout the training. This is subsequent to the early obedience lessons. I will create artificial 'flushes' with balls and dummies as well as making use of any natural situations that may arise, such as birds flying from the hedgerow and rabbits running back to their burrows. I will again make sure that strict compliance to my commands is assured by attaching the lead to start with. I have taught the puppy to ignore thrown distractions when it is stationary; now I want my puppy to react when it is walking or running by stopping and sitting every time it sees a moving object.

Tennis Ball

With the puppy at heel on a slack lead as a precaution for the first lesson, I discretely take a tennis ball from my pocket and flick it past its nose. The puppy's immediate reaction may be to try to chase after the ball as it bobbles across the grass. Because I have the security of the attached lead, I can make sure the sitting position is quickly adopted when I give the hand signal and voice command. Once this position is achieved, the puppy receives my immediate praise, before being left in the sitting position whilst I walk out and retrieve the ball by hand. On my return I pick up the end of the lead and walk the puppy away in the opposite direction from the spot where the ball had stopped. Repetition of this exercise over the next day or two will eventually produce the desired effect and the puppy will begin to sit automatically, without my intervention, each time the moving ball is sighted on the ground or in the air. I can introduce more intriguing objects as time progresses and of course dispense with the lead as trust develops.

Tame Pigeons

More tempting situations can now be set up, and tame tumbler pigeons in the rabbit pen can again be utilized for this. In early pre-school development the young puppy has already been introduced freely to the pigeons and has realized their power of escape by flight. My control is now to be added to the equation. I walk the youngster quietly towards the foraging birds; again the lead is attached to ensure compliance to the command and the correct response will be achieved. The instant the birds lift into the air I stop and am ready to use the lead to manipulate the sit if necessary, coupled with voice command and hand signal. Each and every successful response is rewarded with a gentle stroke of the head coupled with soft vocal praise; equally every fidget or attempt to chase is greeted with a swift rebuke. Eventually the response will become automatic and at this point the lead can be dispensed with again.

Other Livestock

Farmyard fowl, the household cat, pet rabbit, swallows, blackbirds and indeed any other wildlife or stock should eventually all command the same self-controlled response from the puppy.

Natural Occurrences

I am vigilant at all times and make full use of all natural situations as they occur. The summer is an ideal time for this part of the youngster's education, as young rabbits will sit out from the hedgerows in the open fields, Wood Pigeons will temptingly drop from thorn bushes to fly away low in front, and every one of these movements I utilize, if seen by the puppy, by insisting on an immediate drop to the sitting position by the young dog. As my trust of the puppy grows and its respect for me strengthens I will need to resort to the use of the lead less and less.

The puppy has soon begun to follow happily at my side when asked; it will now drop to a variety of commands and instances – voice, hand and moving objects.

INTRODUCTION TO WHISTLE AND OTHER COMMANDS

The whistle is an essential part of any gundog handler's equipment; it will help to increase your control at a distance without having to raise your voice with the risk of disturbing game. As previously described, there are several different types of whistle readily available, the most popular being the fairly high pitched black plastic Acme 210½. It is a relatively inexpensive item which, being mass-produced, is easy to replace if lost or damaged. Horn whistles are expensive and can alter pitch with damp or wear, and each one has its own individual sound, which is more difficult to replicate in any replacement. The silent whistle is also a favourite as it is tuneable to your own hearing capability, but be aware that, as it is made of metal, on a cold winter's day it could become firmly frozen to your lips.

The Stop Whistle

When my trainee is sitting consistently to voice and hand I begin to introduce the whistle. A single short tone, softly delivered, is given at the same time as the other commands to sit and the correct reaction is reinforced with praise. The exercise is repeated over several lessons until the puppy will sit to the sound of the whistle alone. I make sure that I keep the volume of the command low when the puppy is by my side, otherwise a foghorn would eventually be required when trying to stop the dog any distance away. The whistle at this point is only another command to sit and look at me; over time it will become a definite order for the dog to 'stop' when it is moving.

The Recall Whistle

A series of rapid pips will be the recall whistle command for the dog to rush back to you from much further afield. One approach could be to introduce it at the same time as the verbal 'Here' command, using the exercise through the gate, but because the distance is so short the series of pips would not have much time to be delivered before the dog is at your feet. I would therefore introduce this new whistle command in association with the verbal and visual recall commands at a later stage in the training, when the dog is working further away, has fully learned the meaning of the stop whistle command and is fully obedient to it.

Dropping to a Shot

For safety's sake, and to consolidate steadiness, a dog searching for game to flush for the gun should also stop all motion and sit at the sound of gunfire. A retriever at heel should also be taught to remain motionless so that it can concentrate on marking game falling when it hears the sound of gunfire. I lay the foundation stone for this as soon as the dog will sit to the single blast on the whistle, by using a simultaneous clap of the hands to simulate a shot. Here again repetition is the key; I will practise the exercise using a whistle or verbal sit command with a clap delivered simultaneously until such time that the dog will stop moving and sit to the sound of the clap alone. The gradual progression to using a shotgun can now be undertaken during subsequent lessons.

CONCLUSION

Control must be developed fully before attempting to teach the dog the more advanced hunting and retrieving skills, where distance between the handler and dog is increased considerably. Unless you have full control with the dog off the lead by your side then you cannot expect to have control when it is away from you, distracted by another task. Your time will be well spent getting this control developed to a high level before moving on. You may be very pleased when your dog is doing exactly what you want, but make sure that the dog also knows that you are pleased with it.

CHAPTER SEVEN

Hunting

Developing the game-finding ability of the dog whilst teaching control when hunting for game to flush or shot game to retrieve. Stopping to flush, whistle and shot. The effect of different wind directions and scent on the way a dog works its ground.

The term 'hunting' as used in this context refers to a gundog's game-finding ability, the way it uses its nose to find air and/or ground scent to help it to locate and flush game for the handler to shoot and then subsequently of course locating dead or wounded game to retrieve. Although this game-finding ability is an inherited natural skill in the different strains and breeds of gundog it does require nurturing by the trainer and also developing by practical experience to turn a dog into a proficient gundog.

The use of all the senses can be modified by training. For instance, if a puppy is given an abundance of marked retrieves either during early development in play or later on when basic obedience has been taught then the nasal senses can become secondary to the dog's highly awakened sight. Children are great at making this happen – they can play with a ball with a puppy so much that it stops using its nose and tries to find everything by sight! Retrievers, spaniels, HPRs, etc. all require good hunting ability using scent location, but obviously each breed may use it in slightly differing ways, whether searching for game to point or flush or for shot game to retrieve. Therefore the training will progress uniquely to the individual puppy, depending on its actual breed and most importantly the work that it will be expected to undertake when fully trained.

QUESTING OR HUNTING FOR GAME TO FLUSH

During the formal training period the puppy has been kept under very strict close control, whatever the breed. It has been taught to be obedient in the same way as any other gundog puppy so that it will now walk to heel, sit, stay and generally respond well to all commands that it has learned, albeit in close proximity to its handler. Its only complete freedom was at exercise time, playing with its siblings or the other kennel inmates in the security of the garden or exercise yard. Now the acid test is to see if obedience will be retained once more distance is allowed, and more freedom available for the dog to take, as the specific controlled hunting lessons are started.

Preparing the Ground

For the first lessons select an area of ground where the cover is short enough for the dog to be kept in sight at all times, and most

Good hunting demonstrated – FTCh Edgegrove Entitle homes in on a rabbit.

importantly is flat enough to get out quickly to the dog should it decide to pull too far away. Scenty ground, where game has been feeding, is best to encourage any young gundog to use its nose and begin to hunt but I make sure that my chosen area has no game left sitting out before I start. It is advisable to walk over the field, possibly with an older dog, to clear the game before beginning a lesson with the youngster.

Casting Off Using New Commands

A new voice command and a new directional signal will now be introduced to the puppy as I cast it off away from my side to begin hunting in search of game. I will now always use the release command 'Gone away' as I outstretch my arm in the direction that I want the dog to go and start searching. Why 'Gone away' you may well ask. I am a great believer in using a term that is logical to me for the situation that its use is associated with; then, even when having a 'senior moment', it will spring easily to mind in the future. If you think about the scenario in the shooting field, when game has just been flushed by the dog but has been missed by the gun or not presented the opportunity of a shot, then I want the dog to ignore that and carry on hunting. Hence the term 'Gone away' is logical – it is something you would naturally say.

Sticky

Having spent several weeks under close control being taught basic obedience the young dog may be very 'sticky' at first and reluctant to leave my side. It is no use me trying to force the issue by walking forward to try to push the dog on, as this could be quite intimidating for the puppy and convince it that

Kerstin begins Magic's early hunting lessons using short cover on open, flat ground.

Teaching Jasper to cast off on release command 'Gone away' and hand signal.

moving must be avoided at all costs. So instead I stand still and encourage the dog to investigate any likely scent-holding cover that is close by. With a little common sense it is possible to find a piece of ground with obvious visible signs where rabbits have recently been scratching, or a warm seat from where you have recently seen a rabbit or pheasant leave. If the trainee is put in the right situation often enough, eventually the puppy's nose will locate a scent of some interest, and become more and more switched on. The tail will wag with ever increasing ferocity and it will soon become more confident to leave me and begin to search further away.

I have to be careful that this re-kindled interest in fresh game scent does not cause the puppy to switch off to my presence completely. However, the previous hours of training and time spent in each other's company should have developed a good bond between us. If this bond with me is strong enough then the puppy will pause its motion automatically from time to time to check where I am. This may also mean it may return to me naturally, when after giving some well-deserved fuss for returning I can set it straight off again, using the command 'Gone away' and a directional hand signal that it is being taught. The reward for the action of going away from me is either the enjoyment of free movement or the location of scent.

Recall

Remember that this recognition of game scent is not a completely new phenomenon for the puppy as the joy of free hunting was ingrained during the early development period in those frequent outings into the countryside before formal training began and so any uncertainty about hunting should be overcome quite quickly. I want the dog to move freely and happily, investigating any scent whilst keeping within a few feet of me at first. Every time that it checks or looks at me naturally I softly but firmly give the recall command 'Here' and by dropping my hands low to the ground in a welcoming gesture encourage it to race back to me, another quick fuss, then 'Gone away' and the dog is set off in the required direction once again.

Maintaining Control

The puppy may be so engrossed in what it is doing – the nose being switched on can in fact switch off the ears – that it is reluctant to run back to me straight away. The correct response can usually be encouraged if I turn away from it each time it looks at me. It will then see my back and, assuming it is being left behind, should stop what it is doing to turn and follow. If this does not have the desired effect then I would not hesitate to get quickly out to the puppy and insist that it follows me immediately. However, the youngster may still be a little unsure of this newly allowed freedom and so should be looking to me for reassurance or, better still, for guidance.

If at any time the puppy appears confused or tired, or begins to lose its concentration on me, then I immediately slip on the lead, give a well-deserved pat and finish the lesson. Little and often is the keynote to success.

Establish the Hunting Range

Once the puppy is hunting freely and developing some pace and speed I will make sure that I can maintain control by extending the use of the whistle command to 'Sit', to now mean 'Stop moving and sit', when it is moving freely at a distance. Two pips on the whistle are going to be introduced as an audible signal for the dog to turn back towards me. Through careful use of this signal the puppy's range of hunting well within gunshot will begin to be established. However, a dog that hunts to the full limit of range under training conditions may cover twice as much ground when hunting in the shooting field so a much tighter pattern should be encouraged.

I have already taught the dog to react to my voice, hands, whistle, and to drop or stop to a thrown or moving object whilst under strict control at heel, but I am very well aware that it may not associate some of these commands with the action required when it is again enjoying the relative freedom of questing in front. Certainly at this point in the dog's training if a rabbit were to jump up and bolt in full view, when the dog is hunting in full motion, then I would fully expect a chase to ensue even though complete steadiness to fur and feather may have previously been achieved while at my side or on the drop. It is for this reason that I have selected the ground for these early hunting lessons with care. I do not want the complication of bumping into game every yard or two, but I must reiterate that I do want to use ground with plenty of game scent on it to switch on the sensitivity of the dog's nose.

Using the Wind

Wind direction also plays a very important part in how a hunting gundog will quarter across the allotted beat to search for game to flush. A spaniel will probably be searching for ground scent much of the time, whereas an HPR will be using air scent to locate game to point. Whatever the breed, it is of course necessary for the dog's nose to be downwind of any available game scent if it is going to locate the source of it. Any hunting gundog with a good nose must quarter across the wind. Therefore if the wind is blowing directly in the handler's face then the dog should work methodically across it in front from left to right to the limit of the allowed range. It should then turn and work back again for the same distance to the left and so on in a fluent manner, seemingly with little handler intervention.

Back Wind

If the wind is blowing directly from behind so that you can feel it on the back of your neck then the dog will naturally want to bore out away from the handler and quarter the wind back until all the ground has been covered. The handler should then quickly walk forward to where the dog previously began quartering and the dog should now be allowed to run out again downwind on to the fresh ground in front, to quarter it back to the handler.

Side Wind

If the prevailing wind is blowing directly on your right cheek then the dog will want to cast out downwind to the left and then work the wind across in front of you in a zigzag pattern from the left to the limit of the range allowed on the right. The dog will work the opposite direction, of course, for a wind that is blowing on to your left cheek. It is important to understand these automatic differences in pattern that are adopted by a hunting gundog to enable the training to be carried out in a logical way. This will help to develop the dog to have a good quartering pattern, enabling every piece of cover on the allotted beat to be brought within scenting range of the dog's nose.

Headwind Taught First

For these first hunting lessons the young dog should always be taught to quarter a headwind to teach range and correct pattern before attempting to work the more difficult wind directions. Therefore I never work a young dog on a side or back wind but always work the ground with any available breeze in my face. It is also pointless trying to further this hunting education under adverse weather conditions. Strong winds or rain may mask whistle and voice commands, causing unnecessary repetition; and windless, dry, hot summer days are especially unconducive to helping the learning process as scent may be non-existent and even the healthiest dog will suffer from heat exhaustion within minutes.

Hunting not Retrieving

For the first few hunting lessons, the dummy must be left at home so that there is no temptation to add retrieving to the exercise. If the pupil is a spaniel then I want it to learn to keep its head low to allow its nose every chance to come into contact with scent, not to be continually lifting its head and looking in my direction waiting for the dummy to be thrown. I already know through previous assessment how well developed the dog's retrieving is and unless it is already a proficient retriever of the dummy then the hunting lessons would not have been started yet.

I will begin to link the different elements of gundog work together once they have been thoroughly instilled separately.

Teaching the Turn Whistle

I make sure that I keep in close proximity to the dog throughout these early hunting lessons, quartering the ground behind the dog if necessary. As the limit of the beat is reached I will introduce two short pips on the whistle (the turn command), which should attract its attention. I can encourage the dog, using low, outstretched hands, to return to me, giving a quick pat on the head and a few words of praise when it reaches my feet before casting it off in the opposite direction to continue searching, giving it a directional wave of the hand and the command 'Gone away'. If the dog does not react to the turn whistle then I will use the stop whistle as it reaches the required distance, and once it is sitting on its bottom I can use two pips and body language as before to beckon the dog back into me. The turn whistle is just a shortened version of the recall whistle. A few repetitions of this sequence and the dog should be reacting favourably to the turn whistle alone and the use of the stop whistle can be dispensed with.

However, the dog must not be conditioned to rely on always hearing this whistle before turning; therefore as time goes by its use will be gradually faded during training so that the dog remains focused on its handler. The dog must learn to use self-control and turn on the limit of its range automatically.

Developing Self-Control

There are various stages throughout a gundog's training when its control at a distance from the handler is being tested more and more. If the invisible piece of elastic that has been carefully nurtured during training is to be maintained intact, then it is essential not to allow control to diminish. Avoid undue haste as the pupil begins hunting freely in front of you; all commands need to be strictly obeyed, and the slightest non-compliance with your wishes must be quickly corrected.

Trust

Further difficulties may begin once the youngster learns to appreciate that investigating game scent can result in contact with the real thing. The trainer must take great care to remain alert and vigilant at all times during these early lessons. After all, mutual trust must be thoroughly developed during the early training if a biddable and obedient canine companion for life is to be achieved. If the puppy at your side is under good control during its basic training both on and off the lead, and if essential eye contact has been soundly developed and the dog is completely trustworthy on the drop when left during the 'Stay' exercises, then there is no reason why this control should be allowed to disappear once separated from the handler.

The puppy's urge to be with you should be getting stronger all the time if the training is progressing properly, even to the point of making your young gundog 'sticky', or reluctant to leave your side and hunt freely away but instead looking back for your reassurance to continue with this new task.

Induced Independence

One frequent cause of induced independence is the over-enthusiastic trainer who concentrates on advanced or long-distance retrieving too soon. If the dog is only going to be used as a retriever then this may be correct, but the majority of gundogs will be used to flush game for their master and continually ranging out of gunshot distance must be discouraged. You will need to develop the pupil's hunting so that it will only search for and acknowledge fresh game scent in close proximity to you, its handler. Pulling away on the footscent left by moving game will also be strongly discouraged.

Stopping to Simulated Flush

The dog has been taught to sit to a moving object during formal training, but that was when it was right by my side. I now want it to stop all movement when it is hunting. I carry a tennis ball at all times, and use it this time not to teach retrieving but as an aid for teaching this extra self-control. I can discretely remove this small object from my pocket when the dog is concentrating on scent, to flick it past its nose in full view and facilitate teaching the dog to stop to a moving object. This of course is the prelude to dropping to the flush of live game when hunting.

This lesson will only be introduced once the dog has developed a good pattern and range and is obviously enjoying hunting for me with enthusiasm. It is to simulate moving game, and as I wish the dog to stop immediately to this movement I always reposition myself between the dog and the place where I throw the ball. Then any attempt to retrieve or chase can be quickly thwarted with my physical interception. I want the dog to learn that it must eventually show complete self-control and to stop to the movement at its own volition, not waiting for my command. There will be times when you will not see your dog flush a rabbit the other side of heavy cover, and if the dog is reliant on the handler's control to stop it then of course when this control is not forthcoming the temptation will be to chase.

To make sure that the correct reaction of stopping is accomplished I will use my control at first and the stop whistle or 'Sit' command will be delivered at the exact time the dog sees the ball. A clap of the hands with the appropriate hand signal thrust towards the dog can also be delivered prior to throwing the ball, remembering always to give praise for correct compliance.

The dog will never be allowed to retrieve this distraction. Every time I cast the dog off to continue hunting after this simulated flush, the command 'Gone away' has more meaning when it is uttered as I wave my hand in the direction I wish to go. This of course is away from the direction that I threw the ball. If there is an attempt to disobey my hand signal and go after the ball then I immediately intercept with my body and the stop whistle and enforce compliance. A quick fuss is given to reinforce the action of stopping before casting the dog off again in the desired direction, away from the ball. Only when the dog continues properly will I then exercise more control by stopping and leaving the dog sitting while I go back and collect the ball by hand.

The dog must learn right from the outset that I am in charge, if control is to be maintained later on.

Control when Hunting

A gundog that requires constant whistling to keep it within range is of little use, and can even be disruptive, in the shooting field. When this type of unruly dog is out of sight in thick covert, riot will soon set in as it learns the joy of freedom without the hindrance of the handler's control. Right from the start I want to strengthen that invisible piece of elastic which joins the young gundog to me. It must enjoy hunting for me, the person with the gun, and not for itself, looking at all times to me for its reward. I must eventually be able to trust the dog as a willing shooting companion and so harsh or heavy handling to achieve this aim have no place in my training methods. With each further lesson the enthusiasm to continue hunting and the sharpness of the dog's response to my commands will grow. I am also careful not to dull these responses by continually stopping the flow with unnecessary commands; each time a command to stop is given there must be a reason or reward that is of interest to the pupil, and it is not just to satisfy me that the whistle still works. Each time a command is ignored the dog must learn that I shall be quickly within reach to enforce compliance; on no account should the command be repeated without this correction.

Footscents

Pulling away out of shot on the footscent left by rabbits or game is a common problem in the shooting field, usually compounded (rewarded) by the owner shooting at game flushed at extreme range; a chase to catch a lightly hit bird is the rewarding result for the dog. This problem needs identifying early as it can occur during this basic stage in an enthusiastic young gundog's training. It is both annoying, due to a broken pattern, and unprofitable, as game-holding ground is not worked because the dog is focused on one particular line of scent. It will eventually lead to complete disobedience if not nipped in the bud during training.

Game leaving its seat will leave a very strong line of footscent on the ground, which on a good day will remain for a considerable time. The dog that is constantly allowed to investigate it will soon learn that if it runs along the line the scent gets stronger as it gets nearer its quarry. If left alone it will eventually succeed in catching up and flushing out of range or, worse still, continue the pursuit by sight. Matters will deteriorate further with each unwarranted success, especially if rewarded by the catching of a sick rabbit. Remember that a dog's nose becomes more highly tuned with experience on hot scent, and the ears can switch off. Blowing the stop whistle as the dog hits a line may cause a temporary respite from the immediate problem the first once or twice it is used, but that is not a solution as eventually the whistle will be ignored! Remember the dog must hunt well within range at all times, whether in sight, when under the handler's control, or out of sight, when it must learn to use self-control.

The Solution

This is not a time for laziness on the trainer's behalf. As the dog breaks its normal pattern and begins to go out in a straight line I know that it is following footscent. I am after the dog immediately, quickly but quietly. I wish to have the maximum impact through my presence when I can catch the dog unawares as it is concentrating on the line of scent. My direct presence and a verbal rebuke should be enough to let the dog know that it is definitely in the wrong place and should stop immediately. Now I leave the dog sitting on the spot and return to the place where the dog previously broke its pattern before re-calling the dog to me. Plenty of fuss for a speedy return and then I cast the dog off again over the same ground. Should an attempt to take the line again be made then I am ready to intercept even faster now as I know in which direction the dog will proceed. I can repeat the same procedure of applying punishment as before. Always remember to reward the recall and make friends with the dog before casting off again.

Correct Timing of Reward and Punishment

The dog can only associate the reward with its last action, which was returning to me; the punishment had already been delivered for the crime when I ran out to intercept the dog taking the line. A common mistake made by some, which is a cause of confusion, is when the handler uses the whistle to stop the dog following the line and then goes out to still deliver the rebuke. Therefore the punishment is now associated with the dog's last action, which of course was to stop on the whistle command. So you can see that confusion and loss of trust could easily have been caused and this would increase the chances of the dog disobeying the stop whistle in the future. So now the dog would not only continue pulling on footscent but would also be out of control.

A Question of Range

A question commonly asked by newcomers to handling a dog that is hunting for game to flush in the shooting field is, how far should the dog work to each side of the handler? The answer is, ideally well within range of the gun. Unfortunately, the ideal is dependent on many different factors, including wind direction, scenting conditions, the type of cover being worked, quarry species, the size of shotgun and, of course, the shooter's skill. The breed, type, enthusiasm, speed and

Game-finding at its best – a difficult runner picked up by Abnalls Cleopatra in sugar beet.

control of the individual dog will also influence the answer. For instance, one of the pointing breeds should be capable of locating and holding birds by pointing for a considerable time, allowing the gun to get in range before being told to flush.

An experienced dog will soon learn to regulate its speed and pattern automatically to take account of nature's irregularities, but it should still at all times remain within the maximum distance which the handler, who is shooting, feels comfortable with. For these reasons it is impossible to teach every pupil to work identically but, until I have absolute trust in my pupil, I try to keep as close to the dog as possible without inhibiting drive and enthusiasm.

ADVANCED HUNTING

A gundog's nose is a wonderful natural asset that becomes more highly developed as training progresses; with experience it will be able to differentiate between the scent of unshot and wounded game, and also locate where game is hiding from varying distances depending on scenting conditions. These scenting conditions are directly affected by air and ground temperature, humidity, wind speed and direction. This will eventually automatically regulate its pace and pattern according to wind direction, scent and quarry species.

Up to now during the hunting lessons I have purposely let my young dog quarter on fairly open ground, directly into the wind wherever possible. This has allowed the dog to develop a fluent quartering pattern in front of me, with only the very occasional turn whistle now being required to keep it within gunshot range at all times. Working with the wind in my face I know that the dog will have every opportunity to put its nose within scenting distance of any concealed game as long as this methodical quartering pattern is maintained. The dog's nose has therefore been educated to use the wind to its advantage, and the dog itself has also been conditioned to work in a specific pattern across in front of me.

Working the Downwind Beat

When I first cast a young dog off, with the wind blowing on the back of my neck, it will probably seem all at sea, trying to maintain the pattern it has established before when working a head wind. To be able to use the nose is impossible now when quartering away from the wind so maintaining that previous pattern will not work. Even if game was located in this way we would probably already have passed it due to any available scent coming from behind us, and so the likelihood is that it would flush back behind and not present a safe shot.

The First Cast Downwind

It is for the above reasons that a different handling technique must be adopted to encourage the dog to find a new pattern. I therefore purposely stand my ground after casting the dog off, allowing it every chance and even encouraging it to pull away down one side of the beat to be covered. The dog may check this outcast automatically and turn on to the wind, but if not, once about 30 yards has been travelled I attract the dog's attention with the turn whistle command. Now, using a low, directional hand signal, similar to that used to cast the dog off on an upwind beat, I can encourage hunting to begin. As the wind is now in the dog's face it should naturally start to quarter the ground back towards me.

The Second Cast

When all the ground has been worked and the dog has hunted right back to where I am standing, I then cast it out again with 'Gone away' and walk quickly forward to the point where the dog turned on its first downwind cast. I remain stationary there, and hopefully the dog can be encouraged to continue forward a further 30 yards to turn of its own accord, or be turned by the whistle, to quarter this fresh ground back to me. The sequence is then repeated. With patience, and also the success of finding game by this method, the dog will eventually settle into a regular pattern and turn and work methodically back of its own accord every time. As time progresses the dog will learn to watch my actions and begin to cast off downwind as soon as it notices that I have begun to move forward again. Remembering to give the dog time to work, I must be patient and not move until all the new ground has been covered on every cast.

Missing Ground

A dog which is continually pushed on too fast by its handler on a downwind beat, not being given enough time to make the ground good, will start to run with its head up and stop using its nose. Eventually it will constantly pull away from the handler. This is a common development with many dogs that are worked in the beating line on driven shoots, when very often the prevailing wind is behind and the line moves far too quickly to allow them to maintain the correct pattern.

Side Wind Beat

A side wind must be worked using the same principles; the dog needs to cast to the downwind side of me and then work a zigzag pattern across the wind in front of me whilst I remain stationary, until it reaches and then turns on the limit of the beat on the upwind side. I can then whistle the dog back in to me and recast it downwind as I move forward on to fresh ground, as I did when working a downwind beat previously described.

There is again a great temptation for the novice handler to keep walking forward, so pushing the dog on too quickly and not giving it time to make good the cover on each piece of ground. This will, again, eventually induce the dog to lift its head and gallop; it may be rewarded for this by bumping into game accidentally instead of using its nose. Its training should be improving its hunting ability, but in this instance the dog will be taught that it can find game without using its nose and control will actually deteriorate as it is being induced to run free.

Hunting Hedgerows and Ditches

I avoid tackling ditches or hedgerows, which would upset the dog's pattern, until I am first certain that we are working as a successful partnership on open ground. Hedgerows and ditches can really put the gundog handler at a disadvantage, as game will naturally have run along rather than through this type of obstacle and the young dog will probably try to follow suit.

It is not always possible to correct such 'pulling' quickly by physical intervention due to the very nature of some of these man-made obstacles. So I must have complete faith in the level of control that I have built over the dog and be positive that my young trainee has now formed a very strong bond with me. The dog must react instantly each time I use the whistle to stop or turn it in the open, before I risk upsetting this control by working the dog out of sight or on the other side of an impenetrable barrier such as a thick blackthorn hedge or deep Fenland ditch. A very hard-hunting youngster could be ruined completely by trusting it in these situations too soon, when disobedience to my commands could not be corrected immediately due to the nature of the barrier impeding my necessary interception.

Wind

Wind direction plays an important part in how the dog works its ground in the open, and now attention needs to be paid to how a dog will work a hedge or ditch using the prevailing wind. I need to position myself in the best place so that I can keep the dog in sight for the most amount of time. When first working a young dog in this environment, I therefore prefer the available wind to be on the cheek, blowing through the hedge towards me. This enables the dog to quarter up and down the hedge on my side, so that it can detect any scent of game in the cover whilst still in my view, before then drawing into the cover to investigate. As any game subsequently found will probably flush on the blind side of the obstacle, I have to be very confident that the dog's steadiness training to game is complete. The dog must be trusted to flush and stop of its own accord; otherwise a chase might ensue with no chance of me intervening. Therefore steadiness to rabbits using the pen as described in the next chapter should be completed before hunting the dog in these more advanced situations is attempted.

Even when the pen training has been satisfactorily completed, I begin by working low, thin hedges which have plenty of gaps, or open ditches. This gives me the best possible chance to keep the dog in sight the majority of the time and also plenty of opportunity to offer guidance, control or correction if necessary. As the dog gains more experience it will begin to adopt its own method of working along a hedge, using the wind to its advantage but checking itself and even double-hunting occasionally to maintain the range and its contact with me.

Hunting for Game to Retrieve

This is an aspect of the retrieving gundog's work that can be forgotten in preference to hours of marked retrieves and pinpoint handling to get the dog out to retrieves that the handler has placed but are unseen to the dog. A gundog that is so dependent on its handler for direction may look extremely well-trained but it certainly may not be a game-finder and is probably not able to fill the bag without help. All retrieving gundogs should have the ability to quarter ground in search of dead or

Clumber Spaniel Sedgehurst Tempest emerging from thick cover. Hedgerows, ditches and heavy bramble can hide a dog easily so until full trust and control has been established avoid hunting your dog out of sight.

wounded game and then thoroughly work out the area where scent is found.

Holding an Area

More dead and wounded game will be found if the dog is taught to work the area of the fall thoroughly. It may seem logical that a dog will stay in the area until it finds what it has just seen fall, but it does depend on the individual dog. Some will find the slightest bit of scent and stay on it, while others will soon lose interest and start to cast aimlessly about. When this happens they are likely to bump into the scent of other game, which would distract them from finding the retrieve.

Search Command

During the puppy's early development I introduced the search command 'There', when the dog was close to locating tit-bits, or scent in cover. This command will now be used every time the dog is close to the object that I wish it to find and retrieve. If I can control the dog to hold an area by command through repeated success then eventually it will do this of its own volition.

CONCLUSION

Humans do not possess the same scenting powers as dogs, and have to find everything by sight. It is therefore essential that if we wish to locate game to shoot and also find everything that is shot, especially wounded game, we must encourage our gundog's game-finding ability to be developed to its full potential whilst still maintaining proper control when it is out working.

CHAPTER EIGHT

Steadiness to the Real Thing

Teaching the dog to be steady to ground game. Description, maintenance and use of a rabbit pen. Introduction to pheasants and possible retrieving complications. Desensitization to gunfire continued.

GUNDOGS FOR FLUSHING GAME

The transition from questing methodically on game-free ground under good control to actually hunting on the real thing is unfortunately a stage in the puppy's education that is often neglected by the newcomer to gundog training. This can cause so much heartache later on when the first shooting outings are undertaken, and the youngster is liable to bubble over with enthusiasm when live game is flushed. It is essential for any serious gundog trainer to have access to live game in a controlled environment to be able to complete the full training course and to establish the mutual trust that will be absolutely necessary when working in the shooting field later on.

Training Progress

Throughout a puppy's early development I have advocated introducing it freely to the outside world, allowing it to build that desire to enter cover to find rabbits or other game naturally. As the training progresses more restraint has been introduced gradually during formal training using the lead, so that now the puppy is under good control both at heel and at a distance. It will sit, or at least remain steady, to moving artificial and more natural objects. However, the ultimate steadiness required of the dog, to hunt with drive and speed yet cease full motion automatically when a rabbit bolts from cover in front of it, has not yet been learned.

Handler Control

I may already have developed sufficient handler control so that when it is hunting and before the dog has made the decision to take chase, I can stop it on command with whistle or voice. However impressive this use of the stop whistle may seem, this is certainly not good enough alone. I must eventually trust that the dog will exercise self-control and stop itself automatically when live game is flushed, especially when unsighted from me, perhaps the other side of thick cover. To achieve this ultimate goal I find the use of the controlled environment afforded by a rabbit pen invaluable. I know that in the pen the puppy will always succeed in quickly finding a rabbit to

Success at hunting achieved, a rabbit is flushed from cover.

flush and, if correction is needed, which may temporarily dent its enthusiasm to hunt, it will soon find another rabbit to keep the adrenalin pumping.

THE RABBIT PEN

To make efficient and successful use of a pen the pupil must enjoy hunting for the rabbits in its confines at all times. It would be of no use to treat the puppy harshly each time it moved a rabbit, as all confidence in this environment would be lost, apathy would set in and game-finding would be deterred. Although steadiness in the pen may have been achieved, this still would not be the case out in the open fields and so the lesson overall would be far from finished.

Be One Step Ahead

The art in effecting the correct end result is in the trainer's ability to be one step ahead of the pupil. Knowing which way the rabbits will be likely to bolt out of each piece of cover in my pen gives me a distinct advantage over any dog. I can quickly place myself in a position physically to intercept the over-enthusiastic youngster should it break cover after a flush and try to chase after the rabbit. I find that stopping a puppy in its tracks before the chase gets underway, by quickly putting myself physically in between dog and rabbit, coupled with a verbal scolding 'Aargh', may be all the correction that is needed. Over a period of time the puppy will eventually begin to stop itself as it sees me on breaking cover. Each time it finds, flushes and stops, whether caused by my presence or under its own volition, I make sure that I give plenty of praise for stopping, before casting the dog off to hunt again. Always cast the dog in the opposite direction to where the rabbit ran,

Get in position to intercept any attempt to chase.

with the command 'Gone away', to search for another piece of likely cover to repeat the situation. If the dog were cast in the same direction that the rabbit went, this may be mistakenly interpreted by the youngster as a signal to retrieve, and the result would be a chase to find the disappearing rabbit and of course more confusion.

Usually the first few lessons in the pen can be quite frustrating for handler and dog. The dog may be so keen to keep the rabbits in view, no doubt with the intention of chasing, that it lifts his head and bounces all round the cover instead of diving in and hunting with its nose on the ground. Conversely, some young dogs may be apprehensive at first and benefit from an initial chase to switch them to hunting mode. However, once the dog realizes that we are working together and that I will put it where the rabbits are hiding, matters will soon improve.

Concentration

I always keep these lessons in the pen short so that the puppy retains the maximum enthusiasm throughout. There is also a limit to the length of time I can keep my full concentration to be one step ahead and, most importantly, I do not want to cause excess stress to my stock of wild bunnies.

Gunfire in the Pen

Once the puppy is hunting with drive and enthusiasm, but exercising good self-control by stopping to each flush, I can use this opportunity to take the desensitization to gunfire a stage further. The modern strains of working gundogs have been selectively bred over a period of time to produce a kind, biddable animal that is relatively easy for the novice to handle and train. This can mean, however, that some individuals have an underlying sensitivity and, if not treated with common

Wild rabbits tuck into the thickest cover.

sense when introducing gunfire, could exhibit a degree of nervousness to the gun. I began by introducing noises gradually throughout the puppy's infancy; metal bowls made quite a clatter when dropped on the floor, but because they were always associated with something pleasant any surprise was soon forgotten, the sound being accepted as a signal for food.

Using this same principle of the puppy's attention being strongly focused on something it desires, I am able to introduce gradually different forms of loud noise, from the clap of the hands, an airgun report, a starting pistol right through to the shotgun, without damaging confidence. During formal training a clap of the hands has been used as a command to stop and pay attention, and praise was given for each success. To avoid surprising the puppy unnecessarily I have left the use of a starting pistol or the shotgun until the puppy is completely focused on something else. Hunting with intent in the rabbit pen is an ideal time. Choosing the exact moment that a rabbit is flushed to fire a shot with the pistol held in the game bag to muffle the sound, I can watch the puppy's reactions closely for any sign of upset before quickly deflecting its attention away from the previous noise by setting off again to find another rabbit.

Types of Rabbit

Rabbit pens can vary greatly one from another, not only in size and ground cover but also in the type of inhabitants. I personally find wild rabbits behave more naturally, tucking into the thickest of cover, and are much hardier during winter and in the heat of summer. Their natural behaviour will certainly encourage a young dog to hunt with drive and use its nose more quickly than their tame cousins would, who with their apparent lack of fear of predators will not hide but instead sit about in the open.

Pen Construction and Maintenance

I am not suggesting that everyone who reads this book or trains a gundog should start building a pen for personal use, but so that you can appreciate why some professionals may be very cautious at letting strangers use their pen I shall describe the basic essentials of maintaining a supply of rabbits in a pen so that you are aware of the amount of work that is involved to produce such an invaluable training facility.

Construction

Wild rabbits in particular will need a well-constructed enclosure if they are to remain captive for very long. It is surprising how half-grown rabbits can wriggle through the meshes of normal sized chain link fencing, and adults can scale a 6ft fence, particularly over the corners, so a great deal of thought must go into the pen's construction. Ideally the sides need to be at least 6ft (1.8m) high if there is no turn over at the top. This height can be reduced if the top is turned inwards to thwart the enthusiastic climber, but be aware that foxes can easily clear a lesser height. If foxes are a problem an electric wire, as placed round release pens, may be required. Whatever the height of the fence, each internal corner should definitely be wired over at the top.

Great Escape

Rabbits are obviously great diggers and so the bottom of the fence should be turned inwards and buried. My own pen has another roll of 1in (2.5cm) wire mesh which is attached to the bottom of the vertical fence and 2ft (60cm) of it have been turned in and buried to a depth of about a foot (30cm) on the inside of the pen. As most rabbits will try to start a burrow right next to the fence, this buried turn-in will have the desired effect of thwarting most of their efforts. However, I have had the odd rabbit that was so frustrated on reaching this obstacle that they chewed and tore at the wire until there was a hole through it, then made their escape. So this mesh in the ground does need to be a good heavy gauge otherwise the rabbit equivalent of *The Great Escape* will be the unfortunate result.

Size

The pen must be large enough to house the population living within, otherwise overcrowding will produce casualties. Whilst rabbits are believed to be social animals in the wild, they can be and are very aggressive to one another when kept in cramped surroundings. If you have read *Watership Down,* which is fictional but based on actual studies of wild rabbits, you may be aware that there is a rabbit hierarchy and it would appear that once an area is sufficiently populated the breeding of more offspring is naturally controlled. Therefore six rabbits in a quarter of an acre pen are ample, ideally being of the same sex.

Safety Routes

The larger the pen, the more natural it may appear to the trainee. But great thought will have gone into making it user-friendly for the trainer, so that if a dog should chase it can be intercepted swiftly. The rabbits within must have escape routes they can take to get safely away from a chasing dog, so that the chase is not continued and excess stress or cruelty are avoided. There must be artificial warrens they can dive into for safety, or gaps through the bottom of internal fences, that they can run through but that will baulk a rioting dog's progress and allow the rabbit to escape.

Daily Care

The rabbits must of course be fit and healthy, so regular access to food is essential otherwise the pen will end up like a desert. Pony carrots, sugar beet, sprout and cabbage stalks, stale bread and bags of commercially produced dry rabbit mix, and access to clean, fresh water during hot weather will keep them right. Be aware that all this food will attract vermin such as rats and mice, so bait boxes may need to be strategically placed around the pen and kept regularly topped up with poison.

To keep burrowing animals on the top is

Whilst restocking the rabbit pen we take the opportunity to test Sally's young Flat Coat for steadiness to the real thing.

a constant battle, and each morning a walk round with the spade to fill any new earthworks is essential as once they get a foot underground the burrow then grows at an alarming rate.

Disease

Myxomatosis is a dreadful disease, which caged rabbits can easily be inoculated against, but as it needs a regular booster to be effective it is impractical when maintaining a wild population, so I have long since stopped using the vaccine. Each year I will now lose only one or two to this dreadful scourge as over twenty years of owning my pen I have had several rabbits that have recovered after developing all the horrible symptoms and it would appear that the subsequent generations of my stock have built up a good level of immunity. Tame rabbits do not have this same resilience and would be completely wiped out should infection break out.

Should a disaster occur, restocking the pen with wild rabbits is relatively easy with two or three live catch traps and a sack full of pony carrots or rabbit food.

Peg dogs

As well as being used to train hunting dogs to find game from within its cover, the rabbit pen can also be used to train peg dogs to completely ignore rabbits running freely past their noses, and any fidgeting can be strongly discouraged.

INTRODUCTION TO GAME BIRDS

The dog must also be made very familiar with game birds on the ground and in the air, to the point that they no longer hold any strong fascination and the dog's concentration is focused continually on its master. A release pen full of young pheasants is ideal for fulfilling the requirements of this part of the training long before being exposed to seeing an abundance of birds flying over a line of standing guns. The opportunity may be difficult to arrange, but there are many keepers and shoot owners who, if approached correctly, would be only too willing to afford this facility; after all, if the dog is made reliable now it will not be disruptive on their shoots later on.

Use the Lead

When introducing a dog to game birds I would apply the same logic as its introduction to live rabbits – make sure you have full control of the dog by the use of a slip lead at first. Little and often is the key so that the dog's obvious keenness at seeing the pheasants gradually reduces with each exposure. Once the young dog on the lead has become used to walking at your side through the birds as they forage on the ground, then you should be able to trust it to sit motionless amongst them for increasing periods of time, hopefully without incident. As the fascination diminishes the lead can be removed occasionally until trust has developed, to the point when you are certain that a chase is not going to be attempted.

Retrieving Near Birds

Once this complete trust has been established and you are confident the birds are being ignored completely when the dog is off the lead, that is the time to try the youngster with retrieving a dummy from near to or amongst the birds, giving lots of praise for success.

If the sight or smell of the pheasants has a stronger pull than the dummy and your dog disowns it, do not persist by trying again but instead continue with the steadiness to game lessons. Usually with dogs that are reluctant to retrieve in this situation there has been some indication of retrieving problems during previous training, but if not do not worry – your youngster will in all probability retrieve shot game quite happily under any circumstances in the future.

Now you are aware of this problem make sure you avoid areas where scent or game would be a strong distraction when giving further retrieving tuition. There is nothing more infuriating or frustrating than when the previously reliable pupil is distracted by fresh game scent just as it is about to pick a dummy, and consequently the dummy is ignored. Canvas is obviously inedible, so may be discarded in preference for an attempt to find the real thing. Not only is control now diminishing but the puppy is also being induced to 'blink' the dummy. If this does occur, it is essential that the situation is avoided in the future until such time that complete trust has been re-established under perfect training conditions.

I have experienced the odd puppy which refused to retrieve canvas dummies after their first encounter with a rabbit, but the common sense addition of a fresh rabbit skin over the canvas not only allowed retrieving lessons to continue unhindered but actually increased the speed of progress considerably.

Hunting Through Birds

Once I am certain that the dog's focus is not on the birds walking about in view then it is also possible to let the dog hunt through any cover there is in search of hidden dummies, or perhaps even for game that is hiding to which it must also remain steady when flushed. This can be done with any breed, as there are going to be times perhaps when it will be expected to sweep through a pen after a drive has finished searching for wounded birds. Early in the season there will also be lots of unshot birds returning to this familiar sanctuary where they have been housed, fed and subsequently released.

CONCLUSION

Although the facilities used for teaching steadiness to game as described in this chapter will not be possessed by or accessible to everyone, the person who is training a gundog for the first time, or perhaps will only train two or three in a lifetime, should definitely make sure this part of their dog's training is done thoroughly. You may have to pay for the use of a pen or indeed help out a sympathetic keeper during the winter months in return for allowing you access to his pheasants during summer and autumn, but I can assure you the time, effort and cost is fully justified.

CHAPTER NINE

Retrieving and Delivery

An in-depth chapter covering all the natural aspects and some problems, both inherent and those caused by incorrect management or training. The natural retriever, forced retrieving, conditioned retrieving, chained learning to achieve controlled perfection versus trial and error methods. The gradual transition from balls and dummies to real game.

THE NATURAL RETRIEVER

Earlier in the book I explained how I assess the level of each puppy's retrieving desire before formal training begins, and progress may now depend on overcoming each individual's problems that were apparent then or as they arise now during training. The ideal gundog puppy is a completely natural retriever and brings any dummy or object right up to hand. Every puppy will carry something, whether it is an object of play or, of course, when given something edible. This does not mean they are natural retrievers, but instead are just behaving like normal little puppies. A natural retriever will willingly bring back and give to its owner any object that it finds or anything that is thrown for it to pick up.

TRIAL AND ERROR METHODS

Ability and attitudes vary greatly from the ideal example to the complete non-retriever, but during early assessment using trial and error methods plus a common-sense approach it can be possible to find some object that is interesting to even the most unenthusiastic trainee. A puppy that is reluctant to pick up can be further encouraged if I put my own scent on the object I am using. I always rub my hands over the ball or dummy before I throw it. In extreme cases a frequently worn welly sock, in need of washing, usually does the trick. Once initial success is achieved I can then build on it by stuffing the sock with a tennis ball, and gradually the puppy learns by my pleased reactions that retrieving is a way of earning its reward.

I never have a problem with puppies that I have reared personally, as I am always careful to keep nurturing the seeds of retrieving from a very early age. Throughout their physical development period I make sure that this urge is maintained by the occasional play retrieve

Tally, the ideal gundog and a natural retriever.

with well-deserved fuss for every success. The puppy who runs straight out and picks up but refuses to come back with the object can be improved later by the use of a confined area such as a corridor or alleyway, although I find that if I leave any further retrieving work with this type of puppy until after basic obedience has been instilled, when the handler-to-dog bond has strengthened, the problem usually disappears.

Steadiness to the Thrown Dummy

This was introduced during formal training, both when the dog was sat and when moving. So having been taught to sit to a thrown object separately from the retrieving lessons, I can now begin to couple both these elements together. Steadiness could deteriorate if the puppy is allowed to collect every object I throw; therefore I fetch over 50 per cent of them myself. I pick the location for these lessons with care, making sure that I position myself so that any attempt to anticipate the command to fetch can be stopped immediately.

Further Retrieves

As trust and competence builds I vary and increase the difficulty of these exercises. After throwing the dummy a short distance I try walking the puppy away from it a few yards before allowing it to gallop eagerly back to make the retrieve. The use of light cover, cart tracks and increasing distances can all add to the interest and difficulty factor during the early lessons. I am very careful not to stretch the youngster to the point of failure, as success is of paramount importance for satisfactory development. I certainly avoid any long-distance retrieving with young spaniels at this stage, as I wish them to retain a close hunting pattern in the future. Their primary job of course, once trained, will be to locate and flush game to shoot, with the minimum of handling, well within range of their handler's gun. As experience is gained in the shooting field then the ability to make longer retrieves will naturally improve. The retriever breeds are quite different, however, as longer distances are more desirable for them to operate efficiently, but for the introduction of steadiness to the dummy distance is not the point of this part of the puppy's training.

Making the Change to the Real Thing

Unfortunately, it is not uncommon in the shooting field to see a well-bred but inadequately trained gundog making a real hash of an easy retrieve – a mouthful of feathers often precedes the bird being dropped and even disowned completely; worse still is the dog that refuses to return with his prize until it is severely damaged. The raised voice of an irate owner only makes matters worse. A careful introduction to handling dead and subsequently live game in a controlled environment, before being taken shooting, is of major importance to avoid any such pitfalls later on.

I start very cautiously by covering dummies tightly with a variety of different materials to simulate the real object. An old coney fur coat is very useful for this purpose to start with; as the skin is properly cured, it is relatively odourless. However, it can still over-excite a young dog the first time it is sent to retrieve it. Again this is where the use of a confined training lane is a boon; I can easily encourage the puppy to return to me so that reward can be freely given, and soon the fur covered dummy will be delivered willingly.

Using Fresh Fur

By covering the dummy with a fresh rabbit skin I am able to introduce the puppy to the real scent; again, over-excitement may be the youngster's initial response. Some dogs may exhibit a reluctance to lift the dummy with its alien smell, although if the puppy is one of the hunting breeds then hopefully by this stage in its training it has developed such a strong desire when hunting for rabbits in the pen that this does not occur.

When I am certain the lesson has been thoroughly learned I substitute a fresh, cold, half-grown rabbit for the dummy. The puppy may react quite differently at first, there may now be a stronger urge to keep his prize, but as I am training in a confined area where I am in control this is easily overcome. I am careful not to snatch or tug the rabbit from the mouth as this would cause the grip to tighten. Instead I gently stroke the head until the grip is relaxed and I can take it gently using the command 'Dead'. I do not repeat the exercise with the same rabbit; being patient and using a fresh retrieve each time will pay dividends in the long run.

Now to Feather

As each shooting season progresses I collect and air dry or freeze dry the wings from as many different quarry species as possible, so that by the time the spring comes they will be ready to use. During early assessment small puppies can be tried with a wing alone, just to test their reaction to it; I do not give them the opportunity to turn it into a tasty chew. Once success has been achieved the wing is kept only for use in later training. I always attach the wings firmly to the dummy with twine, plastic tie wraps or strong elastic bands, leaving no loose feathers sticking out for the puppy to pick at. I want to give it every opportunity to hold the dummy correctly right from the start. If the puppy refuses to lift this dummy adorned in its new plumage, and playful teasing does not overcome the reluctance, then assuming all was well when the fur covered dummy was used, I can attach one small wing to the fur dummy and that can be picked up with hardly any contact with the feathers. Over a period of time familiarity with this particular dummy and the pleasure received by the dog every time it is retrieved will help previous reservations be forgotten. I can then gradually increase the amount of feather and reduce the fur on it until the problem is solved.

Cold game: partridge, teal, pigeon, duck shot in September.

Cold Game

As the opportunity arises I will try all types of cold game as it becomes available, using rubber bands to secure the wings tightly to the body at first.

The standard of gundogs has improved enormously over recent years in terms of trainability, temperament and hunting drive, but perhaps the natural retrieving ability of some breeds has not advanced to the same degree. Perhaps we need to look at what we can do as trainers to help matters improve, as during the shooting season I see some terrible problems with dogs of different breeds and from various bloodlines, work or show, or a mixture of both.

FORCED RETRIEVING

I have trained many working-bred gundogs and several show specimens, a few of which lacked a natural inclination to carry or were complete non-retrievers. Through a variety of methods I have achieved successes, although the worst case took me three months to gain competence. This particular small working English Springer dog was home-bred by its owner, and he later admitted that its mother had never attempted to pick up and bring anything to him all its working life. I was a little confused when he finally admitted this, as he had told me previously that the mother went out with him on every driven shoot day. I wrongly assumed that she added a contribution to the day, but in fact she just enjoyed going with him so much that, if she was left at home, she was noisy and destructive, and impossible to live with, so to avoid a premature divorce the gentleman had to satisfy the needs of both of the ladies in his life.

But success was achieved with her puppy, even with this inherent non-retrieving problem, using a more traditional forced retrieving method where discomfort, by applying pressure to the foot, is associated with wrong behaviour, and reward, using praise and fuss, is forthcoming for the right behaviour. This was some time ago and I now know that there are better ways of achieving success than by inflicting pain. Whilst the method described next does use a certain amount of restraint and force, it is much gentler and easier to see through to the successful conclusion.

CONDITIONING (TRAINING) YOUR GUNDOG TO RETRIEVE

Whilst all the methods described previously, which rely on trial and error, may bring about success it is likely that there may still be some weaknesses evident later on. What follows is an in-depth practical guide to controlled conditioning in the training environment to gain the perfect retrieving dog out shooting.

Assessment of Pupil Before Conditioning

The natural ability of any pupil has first to be assessed, as you may be lucky and already have the perfect dog, but most people who read training manuals are seeking advice for a very good reason. The actual retrieve can be broken down into several different elements and by doing that a clearer understanding of each individual dog's problems can be addressed more simply. For this assessment I would begin with something artificial and easily picked up; a tennis ball is ideal. It is an easy size for even the smallest puppy to lift and its soft outer covering is more tempting than a small canvas dummy.

The Natural Retriever

Below is a description of the ideal scenario and the desirable different elements I would be looking for in a natural retriever by using a 'trial and error' method of assessment of the dog's retrieving ability. This also gives me as the trainer a guide so that I can work on the areas of most concern, and gives me an idea of which part of the learning chain to address first.

1. The ball is thrown a short distance, preferably on grass.
2. The dog sees it and follows it immediately.
3. The dog finds the ball and picks it up gently.
4. The dog returns directly to the handler.
5. The dog holds the ball but releases it when it is taken gently from its mouth.

In Reality

Now if I had tried that with the same untrained dog using a dead bird instead of a tennis ball the result could, and in all probability would, have been completely different – refusal to pick it up, running off to bury it, even eating it might all have happened. The process of teaching a dog to be a proficient retriever in the shooting field takes time and many hours of patience.

From experience, the commonest problem with reluctant retrieving is related to point 3. Most young dogs, being thrilled by a chase, will run after the object to the spot where it has been thrown, or where game has been shot, but then do not, will not and, in some cases, cannot pick up the retrieve. It is no use the handler shouting and swearing at a dog in these circumstances as that is only likely to make matters worse. Good preparation for the real thing is the key to success.

The next most common problem is the failure to return, and poor delivery is all too common also, but fortunately this is mainly handler-induced and with care can be avoided or corrected.

The two most important elements of the retrieve are the ability to 'pick up' the object and then to 'hold it' until delivered to the handler. The latter is the last element of the natural retrieving assessment and should be the part of the retrieving chain that is taught first. However, this will be done only after the basic obedience has been completed satisfactorily. Now the puppy, with full respect for its master, will return happily and willingly on command. It must also be able to remain under control at heel either standing or sitting until instructed to do something else.

The Elements of the Controlled Retrieving Chain

I previously described the different elements in the assessment of a natural retriever; however, the actual retrieve in the training environment, which is under the full control of the trainer, has many more elements to it. All of these can, or indeed in some cases must, be taught separately before linking them all together. As a guide and source of future reference I have listed them with the desired responses and associated verbal/visual commands and signals below:

1. *The 'Heel'*, to be at the handler's side using a verbal command or hand signal.
2. *The 'Sit'*, using hand signal and verbal or whistle command.

Lyn with Boss, teaching 'Sit' and 'Stay'.

'Mark'.

Pick-up, recall and return.

3. *The 'Stay'*, using hand signal and verbal command. The dog remains in this position until released with another command.
4. *The throw,* when the dog is to remain seated (steady) with taught self-control.
5. *The mark*, when the dog is to watch the object through its flight and remember the exact location of the fall.
6. *The send*, using a directional hand signal and then a verbal command before the dog is allowed to move.
7. *The outrun*, when the dog should take a direct line to the object.
8. *The pick-up*, in which a clean, swift but gentle grip is desired.
9. *The recall*, by verbal and/or whistle command, which will eventually be faded out as the dog gains experience and the handler's trust.
10. *The return*, when the dog should come straight back to the handler.
11. *The present*, when the dog should gently hold the object willingly within reach of the handler.
12. *The delivery*, when the dog's head should be up, so that handler can grasp object.
13. *The release*, when the dog should gently hold the object until given a verbal command to let go.
14. *The finish*, when the dog moves on verbal command back to the heel position. This is not just for polish but so the dog is now ready to 'mark' the next retrieve.

Exercise and chain complete.

Obviously any of these elements where the dog is required to respond to commands, such as the 'Sit' and 'Stay', must be taught separately from the retrieving lessons, as correction of disobedience when the pupil is carrying an object could induce other problems.

First Pick Your Spot

To enable this learning process to be accomplished as smoothly as possible, the canine pupil must at all times be relaxed and happy in the environment you are using for lessons. While most of us possess a good degree of manual dexterity, you will soon find that physically trying to get a reluctant puppy to hold an object gently in its mouth, while keeping upright with all four feet and its bottom on the ground, needs more than just the two hands that we are blessed with. So an environmental restraint is needed.

Sit the puppy in a location that does not afford it much opportunity to move. The corner of a room or fence is ideal, as you can then use your legs to make movement even harder whilst the initial conditioning takes place. However, the puppy may show fear at being sat in such a confined space at first and so it is essential that it is happy to be in that position before you ever start teaching the 'hold'. Teach the puppy to sit in the particular corner in the same way that you taught the 'sit' and 'stay' in the open, with positive reinforcement of good behaviour. Only once the puppy is perfectly happy to sit in this confined space can you then move on to the next stage.

First Link of the Chain: The 'Hold'

Using a tennis ball, with the dog in the sitting position, I gently open its mouth and place the ball in with the verbal command 'Hold' given at the same time. Any attempt to spit it out must be thwarted by gently holding the muzzle closed. At first, if I place a thumb in front of the ball, I can feel the pressure of its tongue trying to push the ball away. When the dog eventually relaxes and grasps the ball I then give praise, either verbal and/or by gently stroking the head or chest with the fingertips. The praise immediately stops with any attempt to release or mouth the ball and the muzzle is again grasped firmly but gently. On no account must the dog win by spitting out the ball, which does involve some manual dexterity on the trainer's part with a really difficult pupil, but as these early lessons progress matters will become easier.

Teaching the Release Command 'Dead'

Once the dog has willingly held the ball for

Present, deliver and release on command 'Dead'.

The finish, with the dog ready to mark the next retrieve.

a minute or so in a relaxed state I move on to teaching another command and controlled action, which is to release the ball on the command 'Dead' but only when grasped by my fingers. With one hand still stroking the top of the head or chest, I grasp the ball with the other; again I do not allow the dog to spit it out but encourage the dog to keep its grasp and continue to reward it for this holding action. Finally I give a quiet but firm command 'Dead' and take the ball immediately from the dog's jaws. If the dog does not release it immediately then I push my forefingers of both hands quickly in the dog's mouth behind the ball to effect the release, and then give praise.

Each of these lessons is only five to ten minutes long and they are repeated daily until the pupil is proficient and can be trusted to hold the ball for as long as I desire.

Teaching the Return to Me

The next step is to teach the dog to move towards me while still gently holding the ball. Again I begin with the dog on a slack lead, in the sitting position holding the ball. I face the dog and step backwards just one pace, and after a brief pause quietly beckon the dog towards me using the verbal command 'Here'. Any attempt to spit out the ball as the dog moves must be stopped, so I make sure that I am close enough to physically intervene. However, if the previous conditioning has been thorough then all should progress well and I can give the praise as before to positively reinforce the correct behaviour.

Take It From Me

With patience and by applying this conditioning slowly over time, the dog will eventually associate the ball with the forthcoming

Kerstin teaching Magic the first link in the chain – 'the hold'.

reward and should then welcome holding it in all situations, indeed it will probably watch your hands as they go into the pocket where the ball is normally kept. When this stage is reached then the 'pick-up' is also starting to be addressed.

If the pupil is really keen to have the ball in its mouth because it gains a reward, there will come a time when it actually tries to take it from me prematurely. I try to associate the ball with coming out of the kennel for lessons. Repeated often the dog will start to look for the ball in my hand as its key to immediate reward and this will encourage the behaviour I want, 'taking the ball freely from my hand'.

Current Progress

I now have a youngster who will happily take, hold and carry an object in its mouth until I grasp it and give a command to release. We still have a long way to go before a freshly shot bird will be retrieved in the shooting field, but the foundation is now firmly in place for future retrieving training.

The Pick-Up From the Floor

The initial conditioning process has been completed and the young dog will now happily take a small object or ball from my hand and grasp it until I give the command to release. This developing keenness to hold the ball should now be such that if I accidentally (on purpose) drop it on the floor the dog will immediately pick it up to gain a reward. If that reaction is not instant then a few more days' careful conditioning as explained before should achieve the desired result. Do not, however, think for one moment that the dog will now be a reliable retriever; there are still several more controlled steps to take before this particular learning chain can be fully linked together.

Follow Me

I now allow the dog to carry the ball at heel on and off the lead, but I do not relax and I still pay full attention to make sure that this good behaviour is well rewarded and that, with the increased distractions encountered as we venture out further afield, the dog is not tempted to drop the ball. I also continue with some basic obedience refresher lessons, sit and stay, sit and recall, all of course with the ball in its mouth.

You may think that this thorough training will bore the dog, but of course the art is to make each lesson short, varied and really interesting. Your own personality must convey happiness to the canine pupil and this is where the trainer really needs to think about their own body language, tones and timing of rewards, etc. If the dog is not reacting well then do not be afraid or embarrassed to get a friend to watch and listen to you in action; there is very often a simple explanation which only a third party can identify.

The Final Link in the Basic Chain: 'The Outrun'

I now have a dog that will pick a ball up off the floor, carry it at my side, come from the sit some distance away, sit in front of me and release to my hands when given the release command. Only the outrun is missing to complete the retrieving chain fully. The temptation for many is to throw the ball and trust to luck that the dog will run out, find it, pick it up and return successfully, but to my cost and through past experience I am now more cautious and wish to increase my chances of continuing the previous success, so trial and error methods are definitely not used.

Again Pick Your Spot

I find a nice quiet spot free of distractions for the purposes of this lesson. This time when I get the youngster from its kennel I do not let it have the ball immediately. Instead I just walk out to where the lesson will take place. During this time I can then assess how keen the dog is as it looks up to me almost asking where the ball is. The ball has of course now become conditioned as a reward in its own right.

The 'Mark' Assured

With the dog sitting I walk about 20ft (6m) away and place the ball very deliberately on the ground in a hazard-free location before walking back to my pupil. By placing it in this way I am confident that the dog sees (*marks*) the exact spot where the ball is. If I had thrown it then it may have bounced or rolled next to something edible, into thick cover, or against a prickly object which might cause the dog pain or difficulty in finding or picking it up. I want everything to be in my favour, to ensure success for myself and my pupil. If all the previous work has been thorough then it is extremely rare for anything to go wrong at this stage, but be careful to remember that you as the handler must react in the same way as you have throughout the previous training. Do not get over-excited at this success but handle the subsequent delivery of the ball as you have on every other controlled occasion, allowing the dog time to settle and present the delivery to receive the reward.

Learning by Experience

With this exercise repeated a few times over the next few lessons, and assuming progress is maintained, then the youngster now needs to gradually learn to retrieve from more difficult locations and over greater distances. However, I am very wary of over-stretching the dog to the point where it could possibly fail. This is where common sense must prevail; whilst it may look impressive to send a dog over vast distances, into thick cover and through hard obstacles it really is unnecessary and could be very detrimental at this stage.

Moving on from the Tennis Ball

I am ultimately training my gundog to retrieve game in the shooting field and now I need to begin the transition from tennis balls to the real thing. The first step is to increase the size and then the weight of the object.

Canvas and Other Shop-Bought Dummies
Commercially produced canvas dummies can be obtained in various sizes and may be very practical to use and a good way forward. However, some youngsters do not like the feel and texture of them. This can have a rather negative effect, but I have found that if I have taken an indifferent retriever right through the method previously described it will carry nearly anything I give it. You can also buy dummies with the same covering as a tennis ball, which I personally have not used. My only observation would be that as I am now trying to 'wean' the puppy off tennis balls then this would only be extending that process further. Imitation wildfowl and game, invented in the USA, are now available in the UK but should only be used later in the more advanced training once the dog has developed complete competence at retrieving standard dummies.

Sock Dummies
For this first transition from the tennis ball I much prefer a homemade sock dummy, which is very easy to make and you can gradually adjust its size as the training progresses. The outer covering is an old woollen shooting stocking, which is then stuffed with every discarded sock accumulated in the household that has lost its mate. With a little skill the centre of it can be made narrower than the ends during the stuffing process. The eventual result is something that is quite large, eventually attaining the length of a wild rabbit, with an ideal place to grip in the middle that is soft, with floppy ends, and, of course, it is easy to pick up and carry as it is not heavy. Out of all the dummies I possess this particular type has been the most useful with the reluctant retrieving dog. It teaches good balance and its only drawback is that it is not waterproof, becoming heavy in the rain, and it will definitely sink if thrown in water!

Once the sock dummy has been accepted then it is easy to transfer the dog on to the more convenient commercially produced canvas type by first covering one in the familiar woolly sock. The sock covering can be reduced over time until the canvas is fully exposed and this gradual transition has been successful.

Once the transition to this larger object has been achieved then the work to retrieve real game can begin.

The Controlled Transition to the Real Thing

The young gundog is now at a competent level with a tennis ball and larger dummies. It retrieves well up to hand and with a good delivery, but if there was any doubt in my mind about any aspect of the retrieve when using dummies then I would work to get that right before moving on to the introduction to the real thing, which is described next.

Use the Favourite Spot
To ensure a successful transition I want to make the first contact with game to retrieve as smooth, calm and natural as possible. Every day for a week when I take the puppy out for training or exercise I give it one marked retrieve of its favourite dummy in the same spot. I have selected this particular place not only so that the dog can easily remember it, but also because it has the right amount of cover to cause the dog no difficulty in finding the object each time. A clump of tussocky grass in an otherwise flat grass field is ideal, as the dog will naturally be drawn to it.

The Simple Unseen from the Same Spot
The second week I make sure the dummy is already hidden in that same place and I can now get the dog used to going out for it blind (unseen). After a day or two this becomes very natural, and when I can see that the dog is anticipating this exercise the time is right to substitute a more realistic object, but not yet the real thing. I prefer to start with fur as a covering for the dummy; it has to be attached firmly, with no loose ends for the dog to play with, and should be cured and not fresh. The dog will probably pick the dummy straight up with out even realizing that it is different, and if encouragement to return is given immediately then all should go well.

Skins and Wings
Over several days I introduce a variety of different coverings for the dummy, which will gradually lead up to actual fresh game. Air-dried pheasant or duck wings from the previous season can be used but must be bound on tightly. The skin from a freshly shot whole rabbit, which with a little care when skinning can be taken off in a tube so there is no seam to sew up, can be stretched onto the dummy. Each progression must be taken slowly and at each lesson only use the item once so that it is kept in good condition for subsequent use.

Cold Game
Little and often is the key, and only when I am absolutely sure that the dog is picking up with the intention of retrieving and not looking for a source of fun or food will I try something real. This is where the time of the year will have a large bearing on what to use first. Spring and summer abounds with young rabbits but I much prefer to use a fresh, but completely cold and stiff, feral pigeon or a partridge.

Not Wood Pigeons
I avoid Wood Pigeons, otherwise the dog may get a mouthful of loose feathers that could make it gag and have disastrous negative consequences. I also avoid using anything large, like a cock pheasant, that may cause the dog difficulty with lifting or balancing at this crucial early stage. I do not use game from the freezer as it smells like carrion.

The Familiar Spot
Using the exact spot where the dog has been accustomed to finding its reward in the previous lessons I carefully place the chosen bird before taking the dog out from its kennel. If I have progressed through the different stages correctly this retrieve will not be a problem. I treat it just the same as if it were still a dummy, letting the dog hold it while I stroke its head. I will then allow the dog to gently release it on the command 'Dead'. The bird is then put out of sight in my game-bag and is not re-used. Once I am satisfied with a cold bird I will then substitute it with one that has been freshly killed and is still warm. I take care that it is clean and does not have the additional distraction of blood or shot-damaged, loose feathers that could cause a problem.

Experience with Various Cold Game
Always assuming no problems are arising then as the different types of game become available I will try my youngster with them, but still under the controlled conditions of the training environment, never tempting a failure, and positively reinforcing each success with praise. If all goes well, then by the time that the rest of the associated gundog training is completed my pupil will be more than ready to tackle the real thing in the shooting field.

It is a well-known fact that the easiest way to ruin a gundog is to take it shooting too early, and that first introduction is critical. I will deal with that in depth in a future chapter.

PROBLEM SOLVING

I have worked through the different stages of this subject as though nothing serious ever goes wrong, but of course from time to time it does. So let us look at some of the problems that can occur during this introduction to retrieving game.

Refusal to Pick Up Dead Game, Fur or Feather

Some dogs refuse to pick up fur and/or feather, not just the real thing but even when it is just used to cover the dummy. This is where a little common sense and cunning can be applied and the versatile woolly sock comes into play again. I have found that if I wear an old woolly sock for an unhealthy length of time, particularly in rubber boots, until it can almost walk on its own, it will then appear irresistible to a puppy. I can then use this to cover other objects, as I did the canvas dummy after conditioning the dog to hold the sock dummy. So I begin with the fur-covered dummy and over time the dummy underneath the sock can be gradually exposed, a little more each day, by cutting down the sock. Taken slowly this never fails, and the same idea can be used with a dead pigeon, rabbit or other game, although once the aversion has been corrected with one natural covering then usually other types of game will not be a problem.

Refusal to Pick Up Live Game

The second dog I ever trained, many years ago, was a show-bred yellow Labrador, Max. All the basic training went smoothly and he would eventually handle out considerable distances, over any obstacle, to retrieve dummies or cold game. His mother had been as wild as the proverbial hawk and so I concentrated heavily on making Max very steady. His first season in the shooting field began smoothly; he retrieved dead ducks, pigeons, pheasants and ground game keenly. After beating on one particular drive on my local Fenland shoot, a gun asked if I could retrieve a partridge which had dropped in the open the other side of a drain. Confidently I handled Max out over the water to the area where the bird lay. As he went to take hold of it the partridge flapped into life and began to limp away. His body language immediately changed; my previous steadiness training had been too thorough and no way was he now going to be encouraged to go after the wounded bird. Apologizing quickly to the gun my embarrassment then preceded a long walk to the nearest bridge to get round to the other side of the water when I was able personally to catch the wounded bird and dispatch it quickly.

Leaving it on the ground I walked a short distance away from it before then sending Max back to retrieve. He needed a little encouragement but finally picked it up and returned with his tail wagging. For many dogs this would have been enough to solve the problem, but not with this dog; he refused to pick up wounded game for the rest of the season and despair was setting in. I analysed the situation and concluded the fault lay with my steadiness training, having conditioned Max actually to be afraid of game that ran or flew, so that he never chased. (I now understand that he needed counter-conditioning to remove the fear response and so enjoy picking wounded game.)

The Sock

The sock was the key to success with Max; this was used with a supply of live feral pigeons for the stuffing. The first ones were freshly killed and covered with the sock, leaving the tail and head sticking out. Within a couple of lessons the pick-up was instant and a gentle delivery followed. Next a live bird was place in the sock with the same amount of body showing. Max's reaction changed immediately even though the bird was only able to move its head, and

Avoid using Wood Pigeons, they are loose feathered.

On the command 'Dead', young Chip gently and confidently delivers a partridge to my hand.

he refused to pick it up at first. However, verbal encouragement gave him the confidence to complete the pick-up and accept his reward although he quickly spat it out into my hand on the release command. Over two or three weeks he lost his fear of the live birds and eventually was retrieving them with one wing pinioned by an elastic band. This confidence extended back into the shooting field and he lived to fifteen years old and never again refused to pick a wounded bird. In this case the problem had been caused by inadequate training and so I have never had to repeat this particular cure with another of my pupils.

Damaging Game

Perhaps the worst problem is the dog that until now has held and presented all its retrieves, including cold game, quite gently during training, but on its first encounter with the fresh, warm article bites and crushes it. This may just be a case of over-excitement that can be cured with familiarity, but the dog that continues to damage game in this way will eventually be labelled in shooting and trialling circles as being 'hard-mouthed' ('HM'). I have experienced this problem with examples of a number of different breeds and some were beyond any remedial training, but I have worked with others that have gone on to gain major success in field trials, where 'HM' quite rightly is a cardinal sin.

The First Live Retrieve

The problem of damaging game may not manifest itself until the dog encounters a live bird or rabbit for the first time, having already retrieved a multitude of dead game without damage and we, the trainers, must be careful not to react in a way that will make the situation worse. In the worst cases, however, the dog may bite and damage dummies as well during training and so the trainer will already have a prior suspicion of what is likely to follow when the dog is finally introduced to warm game.

Inappropriately Timed Punishment

Damage to game can also easily be induced by an over-anxious handler snatching the game from the dog's mouth or by raising the voice while the dog has the game in its mouth. I have seen handlers who were so upset when their dog had chased and caught game that they meted out severe punishment when the dog returned with its reward. I suppose they

Gentle retrieving at its best; live game tenderly carried by the yellow Labrador Lowsommer Wisp of Cirus.

thought that the dog would understand that the earlier crime of unsteadiness and ignoring the command to stop was being punished. Of course the pain was only associated by the dog with its last action, which was carrying back its reward of the game caught to its handler.

Experience

If a young dog damages its first few items of game this can very often be rectified with increased experience, perhaps a quick succession of retrieves, as may be possible on a busy day picking up.

CONCLUSION

The slightest indication of a retrieving problem in the ideal conditions provided by the training environment will probably be magnified when out shooting. Game may be lost or damaged. It is essential that the gundog's retrieving is consistently good.

All problems do have a solution but the trainer must be prepared to be patient and work carefully through the remedial training that may be required. Your patience will be well rewarded with game in the bag fit to eat.

CHAPTER TEN

Directional Work and Scent Lines

Distance handling. Teaching the unseen retrieve. The 'Get out' hand signal. More advanced handling on unseen retrieves, including teaching left and right hand signals. Game-finding ability. Training the dog to follow scent lines. Getting the dog quickly to the fall of wounded game. Directing a dog at a distance.

DISTANCE HANDLING IN THE SHOOTING FIELD

The importance of getting any retrieving gundog quickly to the fall of wounded game so that it can be gathered and humanely dispatched cannot be stressed enough. Historically, pure spaniel work simply involved the dogs pushing birds out of the coverts towards the line of guns on formal shoots, where retrievers were seated ready to collect all the game that was shot. Occasionally a spaniel was used for retrieving game that it had found and flushed for its master who carried the gun out informally rough-shooting. The ability to be handled out for unseen retrieves was secondary, indeed unnecessary, as sight and scent lines assisted the experienced spaniel to complete nearly all of these retrieves unaided.

Modern Practice

Many modern shooters' gundogs, whatever the breed, now have to be multi-functional and take part in all the various forms of work, so may not just be kept solely for the traditional work roles associated with their breed. Rough-shooting, sitting at the peg, waiting in a hide for pigeon, wildfowling, beating/brushing, picking up behind the guns on a formal shoot, rabbiting and field trial competition are all enjoyed. It is essential that we are all able to handle our dog out a sensible distance to get it where wounded game fell, which very often the dog did not have the opportunity to mark down.

I will only begin to teach this extra advanced handling skill once the youngster has completed all its basic training in obedience and has been thoroughly conditioned to retrieve and deliver a dummy well. If it is a hunting breed, I make sure that control whilst hunting has also been perfected first, when it should be stopping on command to confidently mark and subsequently retrieve the thrown dummy.

The hands are an important part of the communication process.

Hand Signals

Handling a dog out to the fall with visual and audible signals should not be treated as a substitute for initiative and natural game-finding ability, but just as a desirable extension of the handler's control. Throughout all the early training I have conditioned the puppy to watch my hands as signals for help, guidance and praise. For all retrieving breeds the hands will already be associated with the direction of sending to find a retrieve, as well as sit, stay and heel, which have already been taught. For the spaniel or HPR the hands are also a signal for the dog to go in a certain direction when cast off to hunt game-holding cover, possibly rewarded by the location of game to flush.

The Hands

The use of the hands is an important part of the communication process between handler and dog. This has been developing throughout all the previous lessons; they have been used to give the dog pleasure by gentle touch, and also for commands and direction. This prior conditioning to make the dog look to them for guidance or reward will now help as we extend their use even further.

Teaching the Unseen Retrieve (a Blind)

I want to teach my puppy to leave me boldly when I point in a certain direction and give the relevant command, as it already does for a marked retrieve because it has seen its reward, the dummy, fall out there. But I wish to extend this confidence to situations when the object to retrieve has not been seen by the dog.

Repetition in a Familiar Place

I use the same spot each day to drop a dummy, which the dog has seen, in a piece of light cover that is in a good location for the dog to pick something from without any difficulty. A natural line back along the path by the fence will help the dog go back in a straight line. I walk the dog on at heel about thirty paces before I turn round and then send it back for the dummy.

'Get Out'

The verbal command 'Get out' is delivered in unison with a directional thrust of the outstretched arm, which is already pointing in the exact direction of the previously dropped dummy. I may need to encourage the dog to move with the familiar command 'Fetch it' said before or after 'Get out' until the new command has been learned.

Anticipation

After a few days the dog will begin to show anticipation of my wishes as I turn in readiness to send it back. The timescale of this will vary according to the individual trainee's speed of learning, but is not usually than a couple of weeks. The indication of anticipation may be that as we walk away it continually looks back to where the dummy has been left, or it may spin round more quickly when I stop and turn round in readiness to be sent. Whatever the particular indication is I will know that the time is now right to progress, and the next day I can attempt to move the exercise on a stage further.

The First Unseen

The following day, unseen by the dog, I shall carefully go and hide the dummy in the exact spot that I have dropped it on previous days. I will then fetch the dog from the kennel and proceed with it at heel, past the spot where the dummy is hidden. If my previous assessment is correct then the puppy should still show some sign of anticipation as I turn as before, even though it has not seen the dummy dropped on this occasion. It should immediately go out to the familiar area when I turn and send it back using the hand signal and verbal command.

If Failure Occurs

Only success will produce progress, so if the dog fails to understand what is required when I give the 'Get out' command, perhaps not leaving my side or just going a short way and then coming back, I will stop trying immediately. Not being disheartened, and to give the dog its confidence back immediately, I will revert to the previous simplified procedure of letting it see the dummy placed. I will continue this for a few more days to build the puppy's confidence and response to the commands before trying the 'unseen' again.

Success Achieved

Eventually the penny will drop, and a confident gallop out on command to return triumphant will soon be the satisfying result. I can now build on this extra trust and the puppy's developed self-confidence, but patience must prevail as although the will to return to this familiar spot each time I ask may be instant, the command definitely has not yet been learned fully in all situations or environments.

The New Location

I can carefully test the reaction to a new location, again where the dummy has been placed without the puppy's knowledge. The puppy will probably look confused when I first give the command to 'Get out' in the new location. Therefore I will repeat the previous procedure of letting the pup see me placing the dummy for a few days using this new location, until I again achieve success. I do not want to upset the puppy by advancing too quickly – only success will breed success – so I keep using new locations until the commands have been learned.

The 'Get Out' Hand Signal

I now wish to teach the puppy to respond to another variation of the hand signal to go out for a retrieve. This is used when the dog is stopped some distance away, in order to make it run away to search further out. Having dropped a dummy on open ground behind us,

The correct response by Rory to a clear 'Get out' hand signal.

I walk my pupil away for some fifteen paces, and put it in the sitting position. Using the 'Stay' command I leave it while I continue walking on a short distance before turning to face it. I raise my arm vertically above my head with the open palm of my hand facing the dog. As I deliver the verbal command 'Get out' I simultaneously thrust the hand forward and down. Hopefully the dog will move away, or a least turn its head, and will look behind to see the dummy lying in full view, and with my further encouragement will accomplish the retrieve.

Associating the Stop Whistle with the Hand Signal

After a few repetitions the retrieve should be gathered consistently. I can then vary the exercise further by calling the dog from the sitting position towards me. After it has come a little way I then use a hand signal and the whistle command to sit the dog. Now I repeat the hand signal and verbal command 'Get out' to send the dog back to retrieve. I take each step a little at a time, as every variation needs accomplishing well before increasing the difficulty, to maintain a youngster's enthusiasm.

More Advanced Handling on Unseen Retrieves

My young gundog will now stop at a distance on the whistle, albeit when coming towards me, and will push further out on visual and verbal commands to search for an unseen retrieve. However, should the pupil deviate to either side instead of going straight back then at present I have no power to correct this, other than stopping, recalling and trying again, which will not boost any dog's confidence. I therefore need to be able to move the dog left or right as well.

For some breeds, particularly those used

A distraction thrown to the left.

The correct response to the right-hand signal, distraction ignored.

for flushing game, the hunting lessons in the rabbit pen or on open ground will have conditioned the dog to go in the direction that my hands have pointed as contact with game, or fresh game scent, has been the enjoyable result on many occasions. This previous conditioning can now be used to assist me when teaching these more advanced handling skills for the hunting breeds on unseen retrieves.

Trial and Error

By hiding a dummy and then sending the dog out from my side, the first time the dog deviates off the straight line I can use the whistle to stop it and then try an appropriate hand signal, left or right, to correct it. Exceptionally intelligent puppies can react favourably to this trial and error method, going instinctively in the required direction, and if a successful retrieve is quickly accomplished this will of course reinforce their actions. I am delighted when this happens, as the reinforcement will ensure that the success will probably be repeated on subsequent occasions and this will enable very swift progress.

However, I have only had a couple of dogs that reacted naturally in this way and I assure you from my experience this 'trial and error' method does not work for the majority of trainees. Most are unable to understand what is required; they will have just been stopped on the whistle and will not see my arm outstretched as having any definite meaning when used in this different way. Most dogs will definitely need a more formal course to attain these refined handling skills.

Teaching Left and Right Hand Signals

Trusting to luck or trial and error is not the correct way forward if reliable handling is to be taught and firmly instilled.

Going Right

I begin this more structured approach by sitting the dog down and leaving it five paces in front of me. I throw a dummy out to the right and make sure the dog's attention is again focused on me by giving a pip on the whistle before I give a clear visible signal with my right arm and a verbal command to send the dog to retrieve. I fully extend my right arm as I lean my body with a side-step in the same direction. With the verbal command 'Fetch it' I release the dog from the sitting position to go out for the retrieve.

Using a Distraction

After two or three repetitions I then replicate the procedure with the dog sitting on the same spot, but this time after I have thrown the dummy to the right I subsequently throw a second dummy to the left. This is not going to be retrieved under any circumstances, but only used as a distraction. I give the visual and verbal commands to send the dog as before for the right-hand dummy. Any attempt to go to the left must be thwarted immediately by voice, whistle and physical presence if necessary. I will then re-seat the puppy on the original spot and, moving to a closer position, I will give the right arm signal again. When success has been achieved and the correct dummy has been retrieved I then collect the other myself and set the exercise up from the start again. Repeating this exercise a few times not only sharpens up my own reactions if the dog tries to go the wrong way but also teaches the dog to concentrate fully on me and watch my visible signals intently.

Going Left

When the dog is responding reliably, every time, to my right-hand command then I can reverse the procedure to teach the left-hand signal in the same way. I want the dog to be very responsive to taking these new orders and so they are gradually taught in short lessons over a period of time. The fun factor is then kept alive and boredom does not set in with the obvious, but necessary, repetition of the same exercise. If I recognize the early signs of boredom then a few more lively lessons, such as hunting in the pen, swimming or just time-out for a play, will soon regenerate enthusiasm.

Combining Both Directions

Once the right and left commands are being consistently obeyed I can move the puppy on further. I tend to use the same spot as before for this so that no new environmental factors or distractions can cause disruption to the training. The next time I throw one dummy to the right I follow it up immediately by throwing another to the left as before. I now send the dog as before to retrieve the right dummy first, but after this has been delivered and the dog re-seated, I then throw this dummy back out to the right. When I subsequently give the left-hand signal the dog, having just watched the dummy thrown back to the right, will not only have to use its memory to remember the dummy on the left side but will now definitely have to respond correctly to my left-hand signal if it is going to pick the one I want.

Once this small but significant variation is accomplished I am now in a position to ring the changes, to stretch the learning process further. I can use two or more dummies on each side and will not always replace the dummy that has just been retrieved on the same side, but may throw it to the other side. Having the luxury of several dummies out, I can always send the dog to the opposite side from where the last dummy was thrown. Sounds a little complicated, but the way to make sure you get it right is to actually simulate the lesson with a friend being the trainer and you in the position of the dog, so that the procedure is perfectly clear in your own mind before teaching the dog.

Never Pick the Last One

It is important that when two or more dummies have been thrown out in any of the retrieving lessons, the young dog is never sent for the last one that fell. This is the most tempting and if the dog is continually allowed to retrieve that one its memory will never be developed and unsteadiness, incorrect anticipation of being sent and eventually 'running in' could be the disastrous result.

Unseen Retrieves on Each Side

As when first taught with a straight, single unseen the principle is the same for unseen dummies to the left and right. Again using the same familiar spot where the left- and right-hand signals have been taught, I will hide dummies in the positions where they were usually thrown, before bringing the dog out from the kennel for the lesson. If the previous work has been thorough then apart from perhaps a minor hesitation when first sent all should go according to plan. I do not make the distance from the dog to the dummies more than a few feet at first, so that success is gained easily.

Right, Left and Centre

Once these extra difficulties are accepted and the dog is responding to my left and right directional signals immediately with confidence, it is time to revise the previous 'Get out' lessons which involved sending the dog straight back for an unseen retrieve, and finally incorporate all three directional exercises into one training routine.

Marked Retrieves

I start this three-direction routine using all marked retrieves for simplicity and confidence building. I sit the dog down on that same spot and having backed a few steps away I throw one dummy out over its head to land a few yards behind it. I now throw one to the dog's right and one to the left. Using the verbal command and visible hand signal to go straight out away from me, I send the dog for the one behind it first. You must expect attempts to go left or right to occur, as these were the last dummies that the dog saw and would be more likely to remember. The dog must not be allowed to succeed in fetching either of them, otherwise the bad behaviour, having been rewarded, will be likely to be repeated. I make sure that the whistle is ready in my mouth to stop the dog immediately if it begins to move in the wrong direction. If the dog disregards the stop whistle I will intercept this disobedience physically and regain

The three-dummy exercise to confirm hand signals have been learned.

control before picking up all the dummies and starting the routine again. When the dog picks the one behind correctly then I make sure it is fully rewarded. I replace it immediately after delivery and after re-seating the dog back on the spot I send it for one of the side dummies – remember, every success will consolidate the learning process.

Confirming Progress

The acid test comes a few lessons later when I place the one behind as an unseen and then throw marked retrieves to the left and right. I send the dog back for the hidden dummy first. If I can push the dog out for this blind and it is retrieved with confidence then I am satisfied that all the directional commands have now been thoroughly learned.

Enforcing Compliance

During future training lessons, should a deviation from the intended line out to a previously hidden dummy occur, I now have the extra control to stop the dog on the whistle and can use the appropriate directional hand signals to put it back on to the correct course; each time that the dog succeeds in finding the dummy after I have re-directed it will reinforce its response to the directional commands I have used to get it there.

If a dog is pushed along too quickly then confusion will hinder its progress. If failures occur or the dog is allowed to pick the wrong dummies, then the result would be a very disheartened pupil that becomes unreceptive to learning. It is for these reasons that I spread the lessons over several weeks, with only gradually increasing difficulty, so that continual assessment of the puppy's development can be carried out.

GAME FINDING AND TAKING SCENT LINES

Game-finding ability in any type of gundog is of paramount importance. Although precision handling has been fully described this does not replace the natural ability that well-bred gundogs possess to locate and find game using scent or, indeed, their own initiative.

The precision handling is only necessary to get a gundog quickly to the area of the fall of wounded game when its own game-finding ability should be allowed to take over.

The well-bred working gundog will develop its predatory instincts and track game by scent if allowed to free-hunt unrestrained by a handler. So many such wild specimens can unfortunately be seen out disrupting shoots. They put their noses down and charge away on scent lines oblivious to their owner's remonstrations. They will flush game out of range from the guns, although not surprisingly some of these recalcitrant animals have built up legendary reputations for retrieving runners.

For the sake of safe shooting practice and harmony in company, and to maintain good control and ground treatment, my gundogs are stopped from pulling forward on foot-scent left by game moving ahead whilst quartering the ground in front of me. There will come a time in the future when not only will my gundog have to follow the line of wounded game, but also it will be desirable that it should follow the line of unwounded ground game, unaided by me, from the seat where it was flushed to the area where it was shot or wounded to effect a speedy retrieve. Its highly sensitive nose will become more tuned in as training progresses and practical experience on the real thing is gained.

I begin laying the foundation for taking scent lines very early in a puppy's life, with simple retrieves of a tennis ball rolled across a damp lawn. Unrestrained by obedience the puppy will soon begin to follow the path of a ball automatically with its nose once the ball disappears from sight as it is rolled a little further away each time. Throughout subsequent training this exercise can be repeated with increasing difficulty, but I make sure that success is always achieved. Night time can add a new dimension; unable to use its eyes the puppy is now forced to use its nose if it is to retrieve its prize and also earn my praise.

As the other lessons progress, and when its retrieving is well advanced in all other departments, then fur- or feather-covered dummies can be substituted for the ball once it has come to a stop but great care must be taken not to foul the line left by the ball with your own scent.

Laying a Scent Line

With care a scent line can be laid on fresh ground without fouling it with your own foot-scent. A fishing rod is a handy tool to enable me to lay a wavy line across short grass with a dummy, and eventually I can use an item of fresh game. I could just drag it behind me but this would perhaps condition the dog to follow my foot-scent instead of the scent of the object. It has of course been inclined to do this during normal training when I have been dropping a dummy for a memory exercise, then walking on and after some distance sending the dog back for it.

The Fishing Rod Method

The method of laying a trail using the fishing rod is simple, but you do need a fairly stiff rod and strong line, depending on the weight of the object attached. I attach the end of the line to a rabbit skin, and to avoid my foot-scent being near the object I drop it a little way out on to open, preferably damp, short grass with an underarm cast. I can now move away, paying out line as I walk in a large semi-circle to finish the desired distance away from it. This distance is dependent on how accomplished the individual trainee is at taking a line at this point in time. As I reel in the rabbit skin over the unsoiled ground to lay the scent line, I can move the rod left and right to create a wavy line or keep it straight for the less accomplished dog to follow.

Once the rabbit skin has been reeled to within a rod's length I swing it in to me and then throw a fresh rabbit back to the spot where the skin left contact with the ground. Without too much delay the young gundog is brought from the kennel and directed on to the spot where the scent trail begins. I use the search command 'There' to encourage the dog to put its nose down to search that area to locate the scent of the skin. If the scenting conditions are right then it will quickly find the line and work along it to produce the rabbit. I am ready to stop the dog should the nose lift off the line and with encouragement I put it back on the right track as quickly as possible, repeating the 'There' command as its nose touches the scent. To be successful I must use fresh ground each time this exercise is repeated. If the same ground were used then the dog would begin to pre-empt where the rabbit is hidden and if the lesson is to be thoroughly learned then the rabbit must only be found by using the nose to track the scent line. These artificial exercises are only a means to an end and not the end itself; this is no substitute for the experience that will be gained later in the shooting field.

Experience when Shooting in the Future

Eventually, after the dog has been properly introduced to rabbits in the shooting field, I will only have to send it off with the verbal command to retrieve. It must then be able to use its own initiative by following the fresh foot-scent from the seat from where the rabbit was flushed, to the shot scent where the rabbit has been hit and, if the rabbit is dead, make a clean retrieve. If, however, the rabbit has run or crawled away from the area of the shot scent, then the young dog's nose will learn by experience to identify the different scent line left by the wounded rabbit which it must follow to find its reward.

Scenting Conditions

Shooting at noon in the middle of a hot summer's day will teach the young gundog very little about scent. It is far better to be out with the lark just after dawn or during the cool of the evening as the light begins to fade to make sure of favourable scenting conditions. Guidance or just encouragement from me may be all that is required on the dog's first few attempts. I keep close up with the dog so that this help can be given immediately if necessary as it works along the line.

Running Pheasants

No amount of training on artificially laid lines can ever compensate for the valuable practical experience on the real thing, and although many modern shooters will only be using their gundogs for working on game birds, I find any young dog will learn the art of following a running pheasant far more quickly if it has been well practised on rabbits first.

The act of retrieving a bird that has flushed near the dog is quite different from a rabbit moved out of its seat. With ground game the dog has the opportunity to use its nose to follow the line from the seat to the shot scent and then take the blood scent to find the wounded rabbit. It has not needed to lift its head and watch the rabbit away to gain success but has totally relied on the power of its nose. With a pheasant, however, there is no such line to follow from the point of flush; the dog must instead use its eyes after the flush to watch the bird in the air and mark where it falls after the shot. On command it must run straight out to this exact area where it last saw the bird hit the ground before beginning the search.

This skill comes easily for the gundog that is walking steadily at heel and intently watching everything that moves. However, for the hunting dog that has learned through previous training to keep its nose down searching for scent, the skill of marking needs to be developed. Very often after finding game, a hunting dog will stop on the flush but then will turn instinctively to look at the gun instead of watching the bird in flight. Experience may soon teach the young dog to watch the gun for guidance and direction, but with each successfully completed retrieve the ability to mark will improve.

CONCLUSION

Directional work involves a lot of handler control and obedient responses from the dog. This control must not be used by the handler to such an extent that the dog loses its natural game-finding ability. Both skills are equally important and desirable in the finished gundog so care must be taken that one does not completely override the other.

CHAPTER ELEVEN

Negotiating Obstacles

Teaching the dog to jump, from early days as a puppy to bold jumping over a variety of obstacles. Introducing the puppy to water. Teaching swimming and water confidence. Retrieving in and over water. Negotiating and retrieving through hedges, over ditches and stone walls. Revision of lessons during the close season.

A dog will, throughout its life, encounter many different obstacles in the normal course of a shooting day. It is essential that the dog is well schooled in this respect and fit to undertake the task if unnecessary injury is to be avoided and wounded game swiftly gathered and dispatched. For a dog to be lifted over every fence by its handler is not only impractical but sometimes impossible, and can be extremely dangerous when the handler is carrying a loaded weapon. Ditches, many with steep sides, hedges, rivers, streams can all present a solid physical barrier to us but to our dog these can be negotiated with confidence.

JUMPING

During early rearing and prep school the small puppy would have learned to scramble over boards across the kennel door. The height was gradually increased as the puppy grew. However, the secret of success in teaching an older dog to become proficient at jumping is never asking too much too soon. Start over very simple obstacles to build self-confidence. I will start teaching the older puppy by using solid jumps of a height well within its physical capability, always calling it towards me, introducing the command 'Get over' at the exact time it makes the decision to try to jump. It is essential that the fences used for these initial lessons are firmly fixed, as the novice jumper will often land on or cling to the top of a new obstacle before going over. Any movement of the obstacle, which could cause the puppy to slip back or knock itself, could frighten it or at least make it extremely wary and reluctant to try again.

By gradually increasing the difficulty, the puppy will soon be negotiating solid barriers confidently and obediently on the command 'Get over'. Only then will I begin the process of teaching more difficult jumps.

See-Through Fences

I will test the puppy over a wire netting jump, which is still very stable as it is fitted with a solid wooden top rail. But now as there is a clear view through the jump, the first reaction will probably be to attempt to find a way through or round, before responding to my verbal encouragement coupled with the command 'Get over'. I am conscious that if I let the puppy continually run up and down ignoring my commands to jump over, disobedience will be taught as a result. To ensure compliance with the command, a slip lead is quickly utilized so that I have direct control of the situation. By getting over the obstacle myself, I can usually encourage even the most reluctant trainee to follow and jump up to put its paws on the top rail. Then when the dog is in this position I can subsequently place my hand firmly on the back of its neck, which will act as a lever to push against and assist it to scramble over the top. With plenty of fuss to generate extra enthusiasm for joining me, the puppy will gain confidence and progress from reluctantly scrambling over, to boldly leaping without touching the top on my command.

These jumping lessons are carried out gradually over time. To rush and try to achieve too much too quickly is not advisable as the youngster will still be maturing physically as well as mentally and young muscles need time to strengthen.

Wire Fences

When I am confident that all solid obstacles are being cleared with ease, presenting no apparent problems to the puppy, and that the verbal command has been learned and is obeyed, I will then try the puppy over a simple wire fence specially constructed for the purpose of this training. I am aware that any gaps along the top could allow the feet to drop through and possibly become entangled, but it is as well for the youngster to actually learn at this stage that the top will give no support to its feet and so it must jump to clear it completely instead.

I therefore use a length of sheep netting, which has large square meshes, but to avoid injury it is not stretched tight as it would be in the shooting field. If the puppy decides to jump on it instead of over, it will give way and just collapse safely on the ground. I ensure that there is a level take-off and landing point to assist a confident jump and good training progress. Most puppies will only flatten this jump once, then subsequently pick their feet up and clear it the next time.

A coat protecting the dog from the wire during training.

The ideal fence to teach a dog to jump with dummy balanced correctly.

Confidence

I cannot stress enough the importance of these early jumping lessons to reduce the risk of incurring serious injury later on, usually caused by an ill-prepared gundog snagging itself on fences topped with barbed wire. I have heard many handlers say that they do not encourage their dogs to jump over barbed wire; indeed they make a point of teaching the dogs not to try this type of jump. Others will put a coat or game bag over the top so that the dog can get safely over, but this is only possible when the dog is close by.

It may sound as though they are doing the right thing to avoid injury, but in practice I believe the opposite could be true. A dog that is a confident, well-schooled jumper will clear all fences with consummate ease in relative safety. It is only the untrained or apprehensive dog that will scramble over, when it would be liable to rip itself on the barbs. There is no way that you will be able to keep your dog always in sight when you are out in the shooting field, or indeed see how a particular fence is constructed at the vast distances that dogs have to go to retrieve game. So this ability to confidently cope with all manner of obstacles is an important and indeed vital aspect of the dog's training and your time will be well rewarded later on.

Jumping to Retrieve

Further complications can be added gradually during training. In the early lessons my presence as the provider of pleasure had been the strong attraction to induce the puppy to come towards me over the jump. Once it became obedient to the command and confident to get over the obstacle without hesitation each time, I then asked it to jump away from me and achieved the same response. This does not, however, mean that it will naturally accomplish the same height or type of jump carrying something heavy in its mouth. To begin developing this additional skill a retrieve of a tennis ball should enable the puppy to still easily scale a small jump.

A retrieve of a full-sized dummy over a fence is, however, a different matter altogether as the dummy needs to be balanced properly to allow a correct take-off and clearance without hitting the fence with the end of it. Therefore this next stage of progression in the jumping lessons is dependent on the puppy first having mastered the art of carrying a dummy, correctly balanced in its mouth, during retrieving lessons over flat ground. Many youngsters will drop their head slightly when carrying a heavier object, which will cause them to hesitate before the jump and take off incorrectly, ending up in a heap on the nearside of the jump and the dummy, having been knocked out of their mouth, lying on the opposite side. So as with all training, make gradual changes to the type and size of object and make sure the puppy is proficient with the new size or weight before moving on to a full-sized dummy.

Matters will just deteriorate if you rush on too quickly and problems could be induced. I have seen a puppy stumble and fall badly at a fence, and subsequently drop the dummy on take-off every time, refusing to go back and pick it up. Worse still, with the apprehension caused by such a tumble the dog could then take such a firm grip before each take-off that on delivery tooth marks through the canvas covering are evident and the seeds of hard mouth in the future are sown. Progress slowly and eventually your dog will become proficient and clear jumps with a full-sized dummy balanced correctly in its mouth.

Jumping into a Vehicle

Once the command 'Get over' is firmly embedded in the puppy's brain and the correct response is instant, I can now extend its use for teaching a confident jump into the rear of a vehicle. However, up to this point the jump has always been through open air with nothing to impede the landing on the other side. The rear compartment of a vehicle is, however, enclosed and there may be a reluctance to jump into an enclosed space at first. I find titbits a very easy way of abating apprehension or fear, the same principle as teaching dogs to go back in their kennel and teaching the 'Kennel' verbal command.

Practice Makes Perfect

Practice at jumping in many different situations during training does make perfect, and even the average shooting dog needs to have these extra skills well-developed so that it can go safely about its normal work in the shooting field without fear or undue risk of injury.

WATER WORK

A retrieving gundog that is reluctant, or even refuses, to enter water is a nuisance in the shooting field. This can be completely avoided if the dog receives the correct training as a youngster. If the trainee is not made proficient in this respect during the heat of a midsummer's day then it is unlikely that it will attempt to enter an icy pond or river in the depths of winter. Fear is the usual block that prevents the dog's brain from making the decision to enter water. A bad experience the first time water was encountered as a puppy, or perhaps just a general lack of confidence, may have caused this problem. Once a dog has developed this fear it can be very difficult to completely eradicate; it is better to make the correct introduction to water and swimming right from the start to prevent any associated problems occurring.

Introduction to Water

During those early outings into the wide world the young puppy may have jumped straight into a river without thinking the first time it was near to one. Very probably being out of its depth the puppy went under the surface and then frantically scrambled back to the bank

A first bad experience of water!

to cough and vomit anything that it had swallowed. As expected, no subsequent amount of cajoling or inducement would make the puppy immediately try again after this bad experience. It is for this reason that I pick the spot for these first attempts very carefully, making sure that the water is warm, shallow and free from branches or other obstacles under the surface that could frighten or harm. The heat of a summer's day after a good walk is ideal. The company of other dogs who are already proficient swimmers is an added bonus and I treat the whole exercise as a game for them to enjoy together. I can just stand back and watch as hopefully curiosity will get the better of the youngster until following the older dogs into the water to run and play happens naturally.

Sensitive Puppy

Whilst the previous scenario will work for the majority of puppies, a more sensitive puppy may cling to my legs instead of joining the others in the water. I can turn this to my advantage by wading into the pool with the others, as clingy youngsters do not like being left behind and eventually it will pluck up the courage to try to follow. I give lots of encouragement to make this happen and lots of praise for each success. It may only be paddling along the margins of the water but eventually the apprehension will be overcome and the puppy will run into and along the shallows freely. It may come to me for praise or, as confidence grows, will begin to play with the other dogs.

Swimming

The transition from entering shallow water to actually swimming also needs to be achieved very gradually. A sloping, hard river bottom is essential so that as the puppy's courage grows it will be able to gently float out of its depth, maintaining its head above water, as it follows me or the other dogs. This transition is more difficult to achieve for the person who is training a single puppy on its own, as there needs to be a big enough draw to entice the puppy to swim for the first time. Throwing stones into the water may have the desired effect but can lay the seeds of retrieving problems. This may induce the puppy to swim out to the ripples but failure to find anything of interest to retrieve is the negative result each time. I have previously stressed that satisfactory progress when training any dog must be built upon success and behaviours that you wish to retain must be reinforced. Although by throwing a stone in success at swimming has been achieved, the puppy's reward unfortunately has disappeared and so the behaviour has not been reinforced but on the contrary it has been punished.

Let common sense prevail therefore. Find a narrow stream that you are able to wade across and keep walking away from the puppy on the other bank; the fear of being left behind will soon induce the puppy to swim across and follow you, whereupon lots of praise or a titbit can be given as a positive reinforcement.

With care this approach to an introduction to water can be started before formal training has begun. But even once the puppy is swimming proficiently the water lessons are still far from over. The ability to retrieve from and over water, which like a fence or wall is just another obstacle, is essential for any working gundog.

Retrieving and Water

Introducing the young gundog puppy to swimming can be done at any age, but the more advanced retrieving work should not be attempted until full proficiency in obedience and at retrieving on dry land has been attained. Remember that a command must never be given if compliance with it cannot be immediately enforced. Should disobedience occur when retrieving from or over water, therefore, unless the trainer is prepared to get very wet it will be impossible to enforce compliance. The timing of any correction will be so delayed that confusion will arise.

The First Attempt

A puppy's first attempts at retrieving a dummy that is actively bobbing about in the water can influence immediate progress. The dummy needs to be small enough that the young dog can grab it with the minimum of effort and avoid taking in a lot of water and choking as a result. It also needs to be heavy enough to stop it bobbing away from the puppy's open mouth each time it attempts to grab it; for this reason I do not use a tennis ball to begin these lessons.

I throw the first few retrieves into shallow water so that the puppy is able to pick the dummy without going out of its depth; this allows confidence to grow before increasing the difficulty. It also gives me the opportunity to try several different objects to find the one the puppy seems more comfortable with. It can take some puppies a considerable time before they gain the knack of picking an object off the surface. Although the technique required is slightly different in deep water, it is pointless advancing the lesson until this skill has been perfected in the shallows.

The First Success

Once the collection of the floating dummy has been mastered, the transition to actually retrieving whilst swimming can now be attempted. Environmental conditions are important so I use a familiar spot where entry to the water is unimpeded and there is a gently sloping bottom. Choose a warm day, preferably with any available breeze blowing the desired object back towards the near bank to avoid any hesitation by the puppy resulting in the dummy drifting well out of reach, which would result in failure. I only throw the dummy a short distance into the deeper water so that the puppy can float effortlessly out of its depth to reach it at first. Future water lessons will depend on the reactions to this new exercise. I am able to assess the puppy's progress and decide where more basic practice is needed, if any. Some puppies are naturals in water, and if you have one of those you may well think, 'Why all the fuss?'

Floating effortlessly out of its depth.

Head held high and the dummy correctly balanced in the jaws.

The Pick-Up Made Easier

If the dog shows a reluctance to take hold of the dummy floating on the water and after a few attempts eventually swims back without it, then to persist with the same 'trial and error' type of lesson would be detrimental to building confidence. Instead I take a more structured approach, perhaps back to where the early swimming lessons were begun, a familiar narrow stream, with gently sloping banks, that is just deep enough for swimming. Here I can throw the dummy over on to the flat ground on the other bank and after a short pause send the puppy after it. In these familiar surroundings there should be no trouble in the puppy reaching the dummy and easily picking it up from dry land. As the return to me with the prize begins I immediately walk away in the opposite direction, to encourage a speedy re-entry into the water and a quick return for lots of well-earned fuss. Practice over increasingly wider stretches of water will soon make for proficiency at swimming with the head held high and the dummy correctly balanced in the jaws.

I will now try throwing the dummy into the water again. Usually with the extra confidence that has been gained, the original problem will have disappeared, and the retrieve will be seized confidently. Once a puppy displays the ability to retrieve properly from both still and moving water, is able to cope with more difficult entries such as steep banks, through reeds or muddy edges, then I will cease throwing the dummy into the water. I will now concentrate on only giving retrieves from the opposite bank. There is nothing more frustrating when shooting than a dog that would rather swim round in circles futilely searching the water's surface than hunt the far bank in search of game. A few simple lessons during training and a refresher with the older dog during the close season should prevent this situation occurring.

Over-Confident Entry

Over-confidence can also put a dog in jeopardy. Many dogs will become fearless through repetitive training and take huge leaps out off the bank before landing heavily in the water. Submerged hazards, old fence posts, branches or scrap metal could spear the belly, doing serious injury, so try to avoid generating this excessive enthusiasm during training. It may seem amusing to watch but it is very dangerous for the dog.

OTHER OBSTACLES

So we now have a dog that will retrieve over jumps of varying types and from or over streams, ponds and rivers. To now ignore

Over-confidence can put a dog in jeopardy (note the branches sticking up).

other obstacles such as hedges, ditches, stone walls and so on would be a mistake, and so gradually throughout the training care should be taken to introduce all these other hazards. I suppose one advantage of living in the reclaimed Fenlands as I do is that watercourses, including the ditches used to drain the fields, are in abundance and there is no excuse for having a dog that will not go over them. Stone walls are obvious by their absence, however, so this is certainly more difficult to practise early on and I will have to wait until those first outings up north on the rabbits.

Ditches

A ditch with near-vertical sides and full of prickly cover is a difficult proposition altogether but using the same principles for gradual success that we used with training to jump, and that have been used for many other aspects, the youngster should soon be made proficient here also. As with the water lessons, where I made sure that the environmental conditions, such as entry, wind and temperature were favourable to encourage success, I do the same with ditches. Begin with a shallow, dry ditch, which is devoid of any cover that could put the pupil off, such as nettles or thistles. Bare ground on either side will ensure the puppy succeeds in easily finding the dummy each time it is thrown over and there will be nothing to knock it out of its mouth on the return. Over time the difficulties can be increased but make sure that you have assessed the pupil and made it proficient with similar types of cover on flat ground before asking it to go through it in the bottom of a steep ditch.

Stone Walls

As the principle of jumping a wall and its associated commands and actions are very similar to those used for a fence this extra skill should easily be taught. It is not uncommon in field trials to see even the smallest of spaniels, the Cocker, scale a dry stone wall which is much higher than its handler and scramble back over with a full-grown rabbit. Mental attitude plays as much a part in the process as does the dog's physical ability. Most of these walls are so high that clearing them without touching the top is not an option, but they are made from uncut stone, which leaves a very rugged surface for even the smallest of dogs to run up and slither safely over the top. I am always very wary when a dog gets to the top and then decides to leap down the other side that serious injury could occur by the dog landing on other stones that over time have fallen from the wall.

Once a type of obstacle is being negotiated easily then, as the training progresses, this can be made part of other retrieving exercises so that the puppy's enthusiasm is continually being stimulated.

Hedges

Confidence to get through a hedge and back again will grow with experience; however, difficulties can arise. I was training a very nice blue roan working Cocker dog for a lady in Yorkshire, and after two or three months he was coming on very well, both with hunting and retrieving. He had a very soft mouth, which was evident when he delivered a dummy, and had never shown any reluctance to pick one up. I was gradually increasing the difficulty of the retrieves and along the edge of my training field was a sparse thorn hedge that was cut right back to the stumps. This presented another natural opportunity for something a little different. He watched the dummy in the air and got out to it through the stumps quite easily. The triumphant return started with gusto; he appeared pleased at having found his prize. However, with the dummy balanced properly in his mouth the opening he chose to come back through was too narrow and due to the speed of his return the dummy was knocked forcefully out of his mouth. He reacted fearfully and ran back to me with his tail firmly between his legs. Another two months of hard work was required before he would again confidently pick up a dummy.

A Block to Learning Caused by Hunting Hedgerows

Although a young dog may have been absolutely perfect at retrieving from the other side of various obstacles that does not mean that the situation will continue satisfactorily once the extra skill of searching for live game to flush from within the obstacle has been further developed. Retrieving through a hedge, over a ditch, lane or track could again present problems as the urge to stay in the obstacle has been heightened by the hunting training and flushing game from within. I find that many young dogs that have had their hunting urges aroused can subsequently be very stubborn at handling out to a retrieve through cover onto open ground.

I have used training lanes and paths as aids to very basic retrieving to encourage a good straight run out and return to deliver. They have also presented a natural line for the dog to follow when teaching more advanced handling on blinds. I now need the dog to trust that my 'Get out' command still means that it must run straight away from me no matter what lies in between us and the retrieve, and ignore any cover or scent on the way. At each change of mind and subsequent deviation or dalliance on scent in the obstacle I must have the control to stop the dog on the whistle to put it immediately back on course with the correct hand signal. This is fine while it is still in view, but impractical when it is out of sight.

Revision

Revision of the above retrieving lessons, with plenty of practice over ditches, paths and tracks with marked retrieves first, then unseen retrieves later will help produce the necessary end result. Once the dog is out of sight I am unable to use hand signals to help should a deviation occur, therefore great care needs to be taken in these revision exercises to make sure that the commands associated with a retrieve, as opposed to hunting for game, are clear. Success also needs to be achieved with the minimum of difficulty to ensure satisfactory progress. The first marked retrieves will be lofted from light cover out over the hedge on to plain open ground so that as soon as the dog's head emerges through the other side it will immediately see the dummy. Each lesson will be made slightly more difficult until I am able to place the dummy out in the same spot unseen for the dog to find easily on command. I now use the same place but reverse the procedure – I throw the dummy from the open field back over the hedge into the cover on the other side so that the dog now has to use its nose and initiative to hunt out away from the obstacle to locate its prize. Frustrating moments later on in the shooting field can be avoided with a little practice on dummies during the close season.

CONCLUSION

The ability to negotiate obstacles is achieved by building confidence through the puppy's early life, then handler control is added later, once good control and obedience has been established in the open. Obstacles create a physical barrier to the handler that the clever dog could exploit to gain more freedom, so work with obstacles should be carried out gradually in parallel with the other training.

CHAPTER TWELVE

Assessing Progress

How to check you are both ready to go shooting. The standards and requirements of the shooting field. How to assess your dog's progress yourself. The assessment process for the Kennel Club Working Gundog Certificate.

READY OR NOT

The majority of the training will be completed using dummies and game in controlled training situations. The dog's reactions to freshly shot warm game or to working closely with other dogs will probably not have been tested yet. Therefore I would not contemplate taking a dog out on a proper shooting expedition until I am certain that all these elements have been thoroughly completed.

During early obedience lessons particular attention will have been paid to those skills that are essential to maintain good behaviour in ideal conditions but this control will now have to be extended to the excitement of a shooting day. Sit, stay and walking quietly at heel, introduction to game, hunting and retrieving have been practised well at home. So, is the dog ready to take shooting?

Minimum Standards

There are minimum standards of good practice required when working a dog out on a shoot, and there is a certain amount of training that needs to be completed to achieve that level before being exposed to the real thing. The handler and dog need to show that they can be an asset on a shooting day and not interfere with other people, their dogs or the landowner's livestock so that the harmony of the shoot is not disrupted.

The dog must be able to hunt and retrieve if required whilst being under its handler's control, and the dog must also exercise self-control when out of sight of its handler. It must be obedient to the handler's commands and, most importantly when working in the company of others, it must have a good temperament.

Temperament

All working gundogs need to be able to get on well with other people and their dogs who they are bound to mix with when out shooting, without showing any aggression or the inability to stay focused on their work in the company of others. This does not mean that there will not be any circumstance arising when tempers seem a little frayed. If a bitch that has been working hard all day is asleep in the owner's vehicle, the attentions of an ardent male admirer may quickly be thwarted with a growl and snap of the jaws. Extenuating circumstances must be carefully analysed before discounting this momentary lapse of correct behaviour. Some dogs may

Handlers and their dogs must be an asset on a shooting day. Keith Dickinson and John Houlton, experienced pickers-up, walking back for lunch at Holme Shoot with gun Syd Pepper.

also guard the pile of game that they just spent time picking up, but it will be difficult to simulate these circumstances to make an assessment before being taken out shooting. However, things like sensitivity to real gunfire can be fully tested.

Control

This is reflected in everything the dog does – whether it is under the full control of the handler and whether it also exercises self-control when necessary. It must be reasonably obedient to commands; I hesitate to use the term 'fully obedient' as we are training a dog for work in which it needs to think for itself from time to time, and a dog that is fully obedient may also be fully dependent on its handler. However, a dog that demonstrates uncontrolled behaviour such as barking when working, or stretches its handler's control to the limit so that constant reminder commands are necessary clearly is not ready for the extra excitement that real game and shooting will induce.

Obedience

This is how the dog reacts to its handler's commands and is closely linked to control. If the dog is told to sit then that is what it should do, and whatever else happens around, it should obediently remain steady and quiet, not moving until asked to do something else by its handler.

At Heel

If it is called to heel then that is where it should remain, closely by whichever side of the handler it has been taught to be during training.

It should be obedient to the command and not need constant reminders to stay there.

To the Recall
The recall is an essential command that must be obeyed. It is used in many different circumstances to call the dog back from going into a dangerous situation such as a road or railway line. It is used to stop a dog going into un-shot ground and disturbing game, it may just be to call a dog back after an unproductive search or be a reminder to the dog where the handler is once it has found its retrieve after a lengthy search. In reality the recall whistle is not used very often, but it is essential that when it is used it is obeyed.

To the Stop Whistle
The whistle commands are varied and the quickness of response is dependent on the actual command used. In reality the dog should stop immediately on the single blast, but that will depend on what the dog is doing at the time. If it has been sent out to search for an unseen retrieve then the obedient reaction should be instantaneous. However, if the dog is hunting and investigating a patch of really fresh game scent then it is expected that there will be a momentary delay in reaction. If the dog is out of control and chasing a rabbit then the stop whistle definitely will not be obeyed. It is therefore essential that all the reactions to simulated scenarios used during this assessment should be near-perfect.

Be Steady
Steadiness is linked to all the other aspects of control and obedience. It is important that the dog is obedient in this respect at all times, and not just when under the direct command of its handler. If it has been ordered to sit, walk at heel, or come back then it should be obedient to that command no matter what else happens around it, such as game flushing, or shot game falling.

Hunting
This term describes the ability of the dog willingly to search open ground and all types of thick cover, thorns, gorse, briars, and so on, to locate live game to flush or shot game to retrieve. The dog has to show that it can do this effectively, especially in those areas where it would be difficult for the handler to find and pick a retrieve by hand. It is no use if the dog does not enter cover willingly, worse if it refuses to hunt when commanded to by the handler.

Retrieving
The dog must demonstrate the ability to find dead and live shot game and bring it tenderly back from any location to its handler as required. The gradual transition from retrieving dummies to cold and then warm game should have been completed thoroughly. The dog is required to keep hold of a retrieve until it is delivered into its handler's hands. A refusal to lift certain objects or game should not be condoned and a dog should not now put a retrieve down other than to re-adjust the balance or grip. When it is handling live game then any hesitation in picking it up or sloppiness when retrieving, or releasing in anticipation of the handler taking the retrieve, could allow game to escape. Game lost in this way is often very difficult to re-capture.

The dog must be able to retrieve from water. This involves entering freely, swimming and bringing the game back to deliver to the handler. Here again, if a wounded bird is put down on leaving the water so that the dog may shake the moisture from its coat wounded game may be lost, particularly in the case of wild duck which dive and will stay under for a considerable time. The dog must also show that it can retrieve from the other side of an obstacle, such as a fence, hedge, ditch, stream or indeed any other feature where it would be impossible for its handler to get to the game.

Assessment Tests
To carry out your own self-assessment of these requirements may involve a certain amount of ingenuity. You will need to set up simulated shooting exercises to check whether you and

your dog are ready for that next important step – gaining practical experience in the shooting field.

For the first-timer or inexperienced novice trainer it may be beneficial to seek the help of those who have more experience to carry out this important final progress assessment. If you have been to a professional for advice or to training classes then they will probably arrange an assessment for you at the end of the training course.

WHAT WILL THE DOG HAVE TO DO ON A SHOOTING DAY?

- It will have to travel quietly in a vehicle to the shoot.
- It will have to remain by its owner in the company of other people, dogs and game.
- It will have to walk at heel to where the drive or shooting is to begin.
- If a hunting breed, it will have to hunt through all types of cover to find game to flush.
- It will have to walk, sit or stand steadily by its handler's side watching game being flushed by other dogs, or watching game running and flying past if seated at the peg.
- It must remain steady after the flush or after game is shot and not move again unless ordered.
- On command it must hunt for and pick up to retrieve tenderly shot game from any location, which may be dead or alive, keeping hold of it until told to release into its handler's waiting hands.
- It must then wait for the instruction to carry on hunting, walking at heel or sitting.

A typical gathering at the start of a Working Gundog Certificate assessment day.

Walking to the first simulated drive with dogs off the lead.

This list is simplified but it will give the reader an idea of what all the weeks of dedication to the young dog's training have been directed towards achieving. Each of these bullet points can be checked using simulated shooting situations, but to be confident that the dog is fully ready you may need to employ the services of other dogs and people. How far you wish to go is entirely up to the individual but the more effort that is applied to making the assessment environment as realistic as possible, the more accurate an evaluation of the dog can be made.

Trial and Error

Some people rely on trial and error, and just take the dog out on their next invitation to shoot or go beating, but believe me it is better to err on the side of caution and make sure that you and the dog are both ready first, especially if you want the pleasure of being invited back again.

THE WORKING GUNDOG CERTIFICATE

The Kennel Club's Working Gundog Certificate's (WGC) preliminary stage assessment exercises are designed to simulate situations commonly encountered in the shooting field. Indeed this would be a useful initiative to participate in, and would enable you to have your dog properly assessed by knowledgeable gundog people.

Format of Assessment Exercises

A typical preliminary stage assessment day begins with the arrival of all the organizers and participants; the gathering of people and their dogs listening to the introductions is

The beating line. Straight would be better!

The 'standing guns' waiting for the drive to finish.

The final exercise, assessing control, steadiness and temperament.

very similar to the way we mix at the start on a normal shoot day.

1. After the introductions and announcements have been made you will be asked to walk your dog off the lead in the company of the other people with their dogs to where the first simulated situation, a drive, is to start. Assessing: control, obedience, temperament and general behaviour in the company of other people and dogs.
2. For the first simulated drive you may have been asked to be in the beating line where, depending on your breed of dog or the role you have trained it for, it will be either be required to walk at heel or hunt in search of game to flush. Shots are fired and dummies thrown to simulate flushes. Assessing: control, obedience, hunting, steadiness.
3. After the drive has finished the people with the dogs in the beating line are asked to sweep up behind the line of 'standing guns', to look for dummies that were hidden before the drive started. Assessing: control, hunting, willingness to search, obedience to commands, working in company.
4. The dogs that were sat in the line with the standing guns will have the opportunity to retrieve those dummies that they saw thrown when the drive was in progress. Assessing: marking ability, delivery, obedience, control.
5. The simulated drive can now be repeated and the participants that were in the beating line can now act as the standing guns. Assessing: control and steadiness. Of course, once the drive is again completed the dummies would be collected as before.
6. A marked retrieve from water usually follows as a set piece, but you may be asked to stand in line with your dog off the lead whilst other handlers are undertaking the exercise with their dogs. Assessing: control, willingness to enter

Receiving recognition for successful training. A delighted Julie Grantham is presented with her Preliminary Working Gundog Certificate by the host of the 2006 Train That Dog assessment day, Richard Green, watched by the organizer, Jules Morgan.

water and swim, retrieving.

7. A marked retrieve over an obstacle. Assessing: willingness to negotiate an obstacle to retrieve and return to handler, control.
8. Several handlers have their dogs sat close together in line, shots are fired and dummies thrown across in full view (a mini drive); the handlers then leave their dogs sitting close together while they pick up the dummies by hand. Assessing: temperament, obedience, control. This is similar to what the standing gun should do after a drive has finished, when they pick all the easily accessible dead birds by hand as the dog waits at the peg.

Assessors

The assessors at these WGC days will have been chosen for their expertise with working gundogs and are there to give advice on any areas requiring further training. If you are successful then you will be awarded with a preliminary certificate at the end of the day and you can have the confidence then to introduce the dog to the shooting field to gain experience on the real thing.

CONCLUSION

It is human nature to want to try out a new toy as soon as possible, and that is the same with the first dog that you train. You have spent hours working through the training, with the help of this book, some videos, classes or one-to-one training and all seems to be going well. The temptation comes with the premature arrival of the start of the game shooting season and you are invited for an early day's shooting. 'You can bring your new dog of course' is the offer by the host, and your common sense goes out of the window. Follow the assessment process thoroughly and any mistake will be avoided. If the dog is not ready but still needs further training, then that is what should be done.

CHAPTER THIRTEEN

The Shooting Environment

The first introduction to the shooting field. How to avoid undoing months of hard work. Taking an inexperienced dog to pick up. First outings for the peg dog. The beating dog's introduction. Working in company and the associated pitfalls. The organized training day. The formal shooting environment.

THE FIRST INTRODUCTION

Taking a young gundog out into the shooting field for the first time is exciting for trainer and dog alike. No matter how thorough the previous months of training have been I am still very aware that this must be carried out with great care. The dog's future role and its breed may affect how and when the introduction takes place, but the principle of using care is the same for any. If the first few outings are done properly then the pupil may not even realize that they are doing anything different than going out for another training lesson.

I have seen many promising young gundogs that were progressing well ruined by being rushed into full battle conditions on a big shoot. Once there in the beating line with pheasants all over the place, even the steadiest dog can forget its manners when out of reach of its handler's quickly diminishing control. As the first outing can be extremely exciting for the young dog it is very important to make this transition from training to the real thing as smooth and uncomplicated as possible, away from the formal shooting field.

A Dog's First Outings with the Gun

There is a great temptation, especially when the end of the game shooting season is fast approaching, for the first-time trainer to take a young gundog out before the training is fully complete. Many puppies start their training in the spring and summer, and although they may seem to be well advanced under controlled conditions it would be a huge mistake to rush the introduction to the shooting field just because the current season is drawing to a close. Make sure that the assessment of training is completed and passed first, even if that means waiting for the next shooting season.

Maintain Discipline

Previous training must not be undone by allowing the dog more latitude just for the sake of putting another pheasant in the bag. If the dog moves when a bird flushes near it then the correct thing to do is not to take the shot but unload the gun and make sure the dog is aware it has done wrong. To have taken the shot would then mean the bird would subsequently need retrieving and the temptation would be to send the dog, which would of course be a reward. Having done this the movement would be reinforced and soon the dog would move a step on every flush. This is just one step away from the ultimate sin of running-in.

Rabbits are Ideal

I am fortunate that the ground I use throughout each dog's training carries a small population of wild rabbits at any time of the year; this rises to 'Watership Down' abundance during the summer months. With all the lessons that have been completed so far, the dog has gained experience of handling cold fresh game; it can also remain under the handler's control and exercise self-control when live game flushes nearby. It is happy for me to carry and fire a twelve bore shotgun during training, first using blanks and subsequently with live ammunition, and knows how to react physically, by stopping at the sound of the shot. It is steady and completely under my control whilst walking or sitting at heel or when in full motion hunting, whether to flush fresh game or retrieving.

Shoot a Rabbit

I can now take the opportunity when it arises, during an outing on the ground that the dog is used to receiving its training lessons, to shoot a fresh rabbit in front of it. Rabbits are ideal for a first warm retrieve; they have no loose feathers to deter a young dog and are a good shape for the dog to balance. The primary objective of this first shooting introduction, however, is not to produce a retrieve but to confirm that steadiness is extended to this new and tempting situation, which will occur many times in the dog's adult life.

Confirmation of Steadiness

The rabbit pen training has previously conditioned the pupil to know that chasing is wrong and so any relapse now out in the shooting field can, indeed must, be swiftly dealt with. A crossing shot of a rabbit bolting back across open ground towards the sanctuary of the hedge is ideal for this purpose; the pupil will definitely see it roll over after the shot. Any unsteadiness, however slight, will not be tolerated. I shall be quick to react to any such transgression, putting the dog immediately into the sitting position and then walking out alone to collect the rabbit by hand.

If any unsteadiness has occurred, no matter how slight, I shall carry on the lesson, but now any subsequent rabbits that bolt in the dog's view will not be shot. However, I will still fire the gun in the general direction but I shall purposely miss them. I want to make sure that the dog is taught full self-control and is fully conditioned to treat the shot as a signal to remain steady when by my side, or to stop all motion and sit when hunting. It must certainly not become a signal to retrieve.

The temptation is to move quickly on to the next stage, when the dog is allowed to retrieve the rabbit, but patience now will be amply rewarded later. I shall keep repeating these lessons until I am satisfied that any inclination towards unsteadiness to the gunshot and rabbits has gone.

The Retrieve

Only when the dog is steady will I let it have its reward for good behaviour, but the retrieve will still be carried out in a fairly controlled way. The dog may be at heel or hunting in front when I shoot, but the required reaction of steadiness to the shot must still be observed. I prefer the dog to sit down instantly at this stage and then remain firmly seated whilst I wait to make sure the rabbit is completely lifeless. I want to completely divorce the action of being sent to retrieve from the place where the dog was when the gun was fired and from the sound of the shot. So I now calmly unload the gun, whilst keeping a sharp eye on the dog to make sure it remains steady, before I call it to heel, turn and walk away a short distance from the rabbit. This scenario has been simulated many times before in training using dummies. After turning and waiting a minute or two, I then give the usual verbal command and hand signal to send the dog to retrieve.

The Pick-Up and Delivery

I must not behave any differently than if it were a dummy that the dog is bringing back to me. I do not want to cause additional problems by telegraphing any anxiety I may have at this moment to the dog as it approaches the rabbit. I patiently wait for the now lifeless rabbit to be gathered and on return I must wait for the dog to present it with the correct delivery. The temptation may be to take it quickly before anything goes wrong, but to encourage a good delivery in the future it is essential that the dog is gently rewarded as it holds the rabbit up. I find that gently stroking, in a circular massaging motion between the dog's front legs, will cause it to relax its grip when I can gently take the rabbit from its mouth on the command 'Dead'.

Retrieve Finished

I will not be tempted to re-use this warm rabbit for further retrieves, as I have found previously to my cost that this can lead to rough and playful reactions from a puppy, inducing disobedience and even hard mouth. It must learn to accept that once game has been delivered to me interest in it must cease. It is for this reason that I give plenty of fuss as a reward for correct behaviour to divert the dog's attention as I slip the rabbit out of reach and sight into my game bag. With years of experience I have developed a knack of keeping focused on a dog at all times; I can recognize the seeds of disobedience and react immediately to prevent it fully offending. It will learn better behaviour more quickly this way than continually being chastised for doing completely the wrong thing, which could eventually destroy its trust in me.

The Wounded Rabbit

I am aware that although the youngster has now gained experience of freshly shot dead rabbits, the first wounded rabbit that it is sent to retrieve may cause surprise by struggling or possibly squealing. This can cause some very varied reactions in a young dog. I shall be on the spot in case the live rabbit is dropped, or disowned through apprehension. Indeed it may not even be picked up in the first place. I will then quickly intervene and humanely dispatch it, replacing it where it was found. I will then walk the dog away a short distance before I send it back to complete the retrieve successfully.

For the apprehensive pupil I will make sure that the next few rabbits shot are again lifeless to increase its confidence before trying the dog again on a wounded rabbit when the opportunity naturally arises. After a success or two the penny will drop and the youngster should quickly return with each subsequent rabbit, whether dead or live, undaunted by squealing or struggling.

Let a Friend do the Shooting

The spontaneity of reaction developed by the professional is not easily learned, as it is the result of years of experience. Therefore I would advise you to ask a friend to carry the gun on these early outings, which will assist the novice and expert trainer alike. It also allows the dog to gain experience of working in company. The trainer is then able to maintain full concentration on their dog. However, it is important to make sure that you explain to the person carrying the gun exactly what you wish to achieve. It is essential that your friend does not tempt the youngster unduly or unfairly by shooting the game too closely. If they are not personally a dog trainer they may not fully appreciate the hard work required to rectify a problem caused by indiscriminate shooting at this vital stage in your gundog's education. A few outings like this and I am happy that the dog is ready to be introduced to working in the company of other dogs.

The Company of other Dogs

With all the youngster's training lessons I have advocated a gradual increase in difficulty

Molly remains rock steady whilst owner Jan Smith is concentrating on his shooting.

in every aspect whilst gaining further experience. The introduction to working with live game on a shoot is no different. Each stage needs to be accomplished well before moving on to the next. If at any stage problems occur then further training must be carried out before moving on. Whilst a dog may have behaved impeccably so far when it is first worked in the company of other dogs, jealousy can cause control to be adversely affected. During training the dog should have been well socialized and experienced in this area whilst using dummies; however, a stronger reaction is caused by the presence of live game and another dog working on it in close proximity to the trainee. It is best therefore to use trustworthy older canine companions for this introduction so that your eyes can remain focused on the youngster.

The Dog Used by the Standing Gun

The ultimate companion for the formal driven shooter is the 'peg dog', where steadiness under the extreme temptation of birds dropping all around it is essential unless the owner is going to suffer the humiliation of having the dog fastened to a metal tether screwed into the ground all its working life. The necessity for the driven gun to actually have a dog with them at all has been negated on many shoots, which have dedicated teams of experienced people with really good dogs to pick up all the game shot.

There is a common theory that it is quite an easy task to train a dog solely for use at the peg but I can assure you that is certainly not the case. A good game-finding retriever used for this purpose may be exposed to several outings every year of its life and it must remain completely rock steady with live and

Sally introduces her young Flat Coat, Purdey, by sitting her well back from the guns, with experienced dog Rory ready to do the work.

wounded game dropping in sight all around it whilst its owner is distracted and concentrating on his shooting. The dog should also be its master's eyes and remember where all the shot birds have fallen, especially those that have dropped well back in cover. The only time that the dog will be allowed to expend energy is when it is retrieving or searching for this wounded game after the drive has finished. To maintain a dog's training up to this standard can take some effort on the owner's part and this skill is to be admired.

Training the Peg Dog

The dog that is to be only used in this way should still have been put through a thorough course of training just the same as a gundog that is going to be used as an all-rounder. The way it is first introduced to shooting will be similar also to that described previously. The mistake many people make is to introduce it instead by sitting it at the standing gun's peg on its first outing to a formal shoot. This action by the owner will certainly lead to premature failure.

The Dog's Initial Introduction to Driven Shooting

Having made the introduction to shooting game as previously described (as an extension of the training environment) and also having worked the dog in company, I would then put the dog in a situation where it could sit and watch a large number of birds being shot at and dropping on the ground around it. This can be achieved on a day's picking-up, although the young dog certainly should not be allowed to retrieve anything that is shot in this new situation for several outings.

I personally have the advantage of a purpose built dog trailer and a mixed team of experienced picking up dogs to do all the work that I have agreed to do for the shoot, whilst introducing a youngster. I can get in locations that

Syd Pepper shooting driven partridges at Holme, with his young dog positioned where he can see it.

are well back from the line of guns whereby the new dog is not put under extreme pressure but it is still able to witness everything that is happening in front. I will make sure that I am placed correctly so that the birds, after they have passed over the line of standing guns, will plane down and be landing all around me and the young dog. Once the drive is over the youngster can then be removed to the security of the trailer whilst I pick up the game with the older dogs. While the drive is in progress, the young dog will be sat a few feet in front of me so that I can keeping a close eye on it and instantly discourage any movement or wrong behaviour.

The dog will only be allowed to sit and watch a couple of drives on the first day and if that goes well then it will be gradually exposed more and more to the action on subsequent days. When I am certain that I can trust it to behave impeccably during a drive in progress, I will subsequently allow it to stay at heel while my other dogs sweep up the shot game behind the guns after the drive has finished. It will still not be sent or allowed to attempt a retrieve itself as complete steadiness is going to be of paramount importance for the rest of this dog's life.

One particular Labrador bitch that I trained as a peg dog for the shoot captain of a prestigious formal driven pheasant shoot was taken out with my picking up team for a whole season without ever being allowed to retrieve a bird at the end of any drive. You may think that was unnecessary, but the dog came to me several months previously completely untrained, ten months old and with an inbuilt desire to chase anything that moved. By the end of that season it could be trusted implicitly during a drive.

Sit the Dog in Front

If you are going to be shooting driven pheasants and it is the first time your new dog has accompanied you, assuming it has been introduced properly to shooting then it is still very important not to let your concentration on the day's sport cause the dog's training to lapse. Always sit the dog where you can see it; out in front of the peg a couple of metres is ideal. You can then easily glance at the dog and keep watch for birds coming your way whilst enjoying a day's sport.

Always Move the Dog from the Peg

Before sending the dog after the drive has finished, the gun should pick all the birds lying in view by hand. Only then should the dog be sent to try for any birds that have fallen or run into cover. However, before being sent the dog should always be taken a few yards away from the peg on purpose. The reason is that you will want the dog in the future to see the peg as a place to be absolutely still, rock steady at all times under any temptation, and definitely not to associate it as the spot from which it will be sent to retrieve at any time.

I have seen many promising young peg dogs ruined by being sent from where they have been patiently sitting immediately after the keeper's whistle or horn has signalled that the drive has finished. With repetition the keeper's whistle will actually become the cue to go and retrieve. The owner, who has been distracted putting his gun safely out of harm's way in the slip, can then only look on in dismay at the dog, which is already returning with a dead pheasant in its mouth. Anger may follow and the situation deteriorates as the dog will have been wrongly chastised for picking the pheasant, not for the crime of leaving its post without orders from the boss! If you never send your dog from the peg, steadiness will be maintained.

The Occasional Driven Day

All my own gundogs, once fully trained and thoroughly experienced, retriever, spaniel and HPR alike, at some time in their life may be required to sit quietly and steadily at a peg, without lead but still under full control. The smaller Cockers seem to be less suited to the pressure of this situation and my shooting accuracy may suffer by their restlessness. The larger English Springer Spaniels are, however, much more adaptable and soon begin to realize what is required in this unusual situation, waiting eagerly for the drive to end and then waiting patiently while I pick any birds which are lying dead in the open by hand. Whatever the chosen breed, only if it has behaved well during the drive will I give it the opportunity of a retrieve, to reward good behaviour.

The Beating Dog

Not all dogs that have been trained to hunt to flush game on a rough-shooting day can also cope with the excessive amounts of game that they may encounter when used in the beating line of a large shoot. Many promising young hunting dogs have been ruined by working freely in this role, but on the contrary if done with care it can be a good way of getting a 'sticky' dog motivated and giving a potential trial dog more experience.

Blanking In

A typical drive will begin with the beaters 'blanking in' open fields into the cover which is going to be the point where the birds are flushed out towards the standing guns. This preparatory work may take place long before the guns are in position on the pegs and in this more relaxed part of the drive a beater with a young dog has the opportunity to concentrate fully on maintaining good, close control whilst moving game forward. When the end of the drive draws nearer, the birds will be bottled up in the flushing point, producing extreme temptation for the dogs to pull forward. This could cause a dog to riot, doing irreparable damage both to its training and of course to the shoot as all the birds would disappear at once, no doubt in the wrong direction. So the young dog should be at heel or on the lead long before the situation arises where control will be stretched to the limit.

Clarify your Role for the Day

If you are going beating then explain to the gamekeeper before you start the day what you would like to achieve with your young dog

Eager show spaniel owners take part in the United Spaniel Association's training day with their Sussex, Clumbers, Welsh and English Springers at Exbury.

so that you are not pressured into hunting in situations in which you cannot maintain control. You want to be able to get out to the dog before it boils over and decides to disobey, so being expected to hunt through six foot high kale full of birds running forward is definitely not a good idea. If exposed to game in this way the dog will soon learn that it can chase the birds into the air when out of your sight, and before long it will be coursing one out across open ground towards the standing guns. Hunting an open ditch or a field of sugar beet is far more controllable and you will be able to get to your dog more easily should disobedience look likely.

THE ORGANIZED TRAINING DAY

This type of day has become very popular in recent years. Like-minded gundog folk join together and take a day's shooting for introducing their young dogs to working in company in the shooting field, and for increasing the training and experience of older dogs.

Many such days are organized by clubs, with experienced instructors/trainers on hand to give assistance when required. They may be tailored to suit the different needs of the people taking part; introduction to shooting, field trials or just to further a dog's experience under controlled conditions. Getting to know of their whereabouts is not easy at first but as many of the keen field triallers take advantage of such days then they are a good place to start when seeking contacts. The Kennel Club has lists of all registered clubs and also all the KC Panel Judges, many of whom are involved in organizing or helping at these training days.

A Training Day

I recently shot at one such day and will describe the experience so that you can form an opinion on the pros and cons yourself. This day was organized for a group of field trial handlers by Phil Garton, an experienced trainer of field trial Labradors who has recently competed with a working Cocker and has a broad knowledge of all types of gundog competition as well as the shooting field. Although the day sounds as though it may be aimed solely at those who were polishing their dogs up for field trial competition, this was not in fact the case.

Guns and their Spaniels

I had been asked if I would like to shoot in the team of guns and was advised that as it was all in a huge field of sugar beet in Lincolnshire full of red-legged partridge then I would be welcome to bring one of my spaniels to assist in flushing the game. Both the six guns and the six retriever handlers each paid a fixed amount for the privilege, so the costs were fairly split. Nathan Clayton and I, besides shooting, also worked spaniels in front of the retrievers who stayed at heel. The hunting dogs were there purely to flush game and were not there to retrieve. The organizer kindly offered us the chance to let our spaniels have a bird occasionally, but to maintain the best behaviour and steadiness we decided that it was better to keep any thought of retrieving out of our two very enthusiastic Springers' minds, especially as my friend's bitch, Caddis, occasionally needed reminding that she was hunting for him and not for herself. This arrangement also allowed us to concentrate more fully on shooting the birds for the other handlers who had paid for the privilege, to train their dogs.

The Briefing

The day began with a briefing for the handlers and guns on what was expected of the day and of them; safety was paramount and harsh handling would not be tolerated. The guns and handlers were evenly spaced in the shooting line at the end of a massive field of sugar beet. As the whole day would be walked up it was decided that the guns would move position at the end of each beat so that each had the opportunity of being a flank gun at some time, as many of the birds would try to escape around the sides.

Shooting and Training Begins

The line moving steadily forward was regulated by the speed of our spaniels hunting in front. We had not moved too far before a partridge was flushed and the first dog could show its marking ability with a slick retrieve. Being a normal walked-up shooting day, the early retrieves were quite straightforward; but even so, for a young dog not used to being in the company of so many other people and other dogs it was something very new for them.

A couple of the young Labradors at first hung back and needed reminding to stay close at heel, but as the day progressed, after they had been able to retrieve several birds, you could see the confidence grow. By the end of the day experience had taught them to watch every thing that flew.

Empty Mouth

One handler had a problem getting his dog to stop hunting and recall with an empty mouth after trying unsuccessfully for a retrieve. The dog was very reluctant to come back in, so the handler was able to pick situations during the day where he knew the dog would fail to pick up a bird, either the bird had been already been picked by another dog or the bird had flown away again. He would send his dog out to the fall area, let it hunt on the residual scent of the game which had already been picked and then made sure it responded to the recall command and returned without anything in its mouth, when it was amply rewarded with praise. This was a more experienced dog and so the failure to find would not affect its training, but having this opportunity meant that a cure for the previous disobedience to the recall was soon becoming evident.

Heelwork

If you are carrying a gun and also have a dog at heel to retrieve any shot game then safety dictates that it should not interfere with you. Some handlers on this day had real heelwork issues with their dogs; some were obviously very keen and kept moving forward. Although

Homeward bound after a successful day's picking up on Holme Shoot.

this put them in a good position to mark, there is a fine line between that and the beginnings of unsteadiness or, worse still, risking tripping up the owner. Again, as the handlers could give full concentration to the training, the opportunity was there to make sure that the dogs stayed in the correct position.

More Difficult Retrieves

As the day progressed the dogs were given retrieves to suit the requirements of the individual. The handlers with less experienced dogs were happy to take straightforward marked retrieves, of gradually increasing distances, to build their dogs' confidence and marking ability. Some of the field trial dogs were fully stretched on long retrieves across the line or on birds that had fallen over the boundary ditches and on those birds that were obviously going to run as they planed down.

Eye-Wipes

The day was a little competitive; the guns were obviously delighted if they eye-wiped one of their colleagues, but of course with some of the more difficult retrieves the opportunity for dogs to be tried on birds that had not been found by others was also there. Perhaps the best eye-wipe was by Nathan's tireless Caddis, who found a partridge that had run off open ground into a dry ditch bottom after Phil's young field trial Lab had found the fall, and searched the area thoroughly but unsuccessfully!

Field trial dogs are very often stretched on long retrieves across the line. David Field sends Artistryn Jay for a hare shot by keeper Julian Bond at the KC two-day open stake at Holkham, 2006.

Advantages of Training Days

That whole day was run for the benefit of training the dogs. The aim was to allow this to take place under very real conditions but because the day was controlled then bad behaviour could be nipped in the bud immediately, something that is very often not possible when out on a normal day's shooting. There was no harsh handling and because handlers were able to get out safely to their dogs when any disobedience occurred then good progress was made by all.

These organized days definitely present an ideal intermediate step for young dogs, creating a suitable link between the first solitary outing, and actually being made ready to go out on a formal day.

CONCLUSION

A planned and careful introduction to the shooting field will help ensure that a lifelong partnership develops. Concentrate fully on the dog by leaving your gun at home for the first few outings and let others do the shooting. Do not let your concentration on the dog reduce once you are also enjoying the distraction of shooting, especially in its first season. Do not be pressured by others into pushing the dog on too quickly.

CHAPTER FOURTEEN

Health and Welfare

Care of the gundog during the close season. Refresher training. Exercise during the lead-up to the shooting season. Kennel management, including cleaning, appropriate bedding and parasite control. A note on heatstroke, both in the kennel and in the car.

SUMMER MAINTENANCE

To keep a dog in the peak of working fitness for twelve months of the year is not only unnecessary but also virtually impossible. Its fitness levels need to be adjusted according to the output required. Weeks of hard work during a busy shooting season, hunting through all types of cover including punishing thorns and briars in search of game, can really takes its toll. I give my own gundogs a well-earned rest and reduce the fuel intake accordingly, immediately after the close of the shooting season when their normal activity levels are reduced. This allows the batteries to recharge and also gives any battle scars time to heal.

Diet

During these less active months of the year I also change the fuel intake from the high performance, high protein food that the dogs have been on through the rigours of the shooting season to a good maintenance diet with a subsequent reduction in quantity, not quality.

Routine Care and Welfare

Exercise, grooming, treating for worms or skin vermin, and yearly booster vaccinations are all essential clinical and health requirements that need to be done on a regular basis to keep the dogs in tip-top condition. A regular daily health check is preferable, which will allow the owner to spot problems such as fleas, lice or ear mites before they have a chance to reach infestation proportions. A routine health check by your vet after the season has finished and at the same time as getting the annual booster done is a good idea to rule out any health issues that cannot be identified during the owner's routine checks.

Refresher Training

The close season for shooting is also a time to improve any deficiencies in the dog's work or training that may have been noticed during the last season. For the less experienced dog perhaps a reluctance to negotiate some new obstacle or further practice in water may be required, but any problem, no matter how small, should be worked on by the trainer before it becomes a major headache. For those owners who are not fortunate enough to be able to devote the necessary time and have opted previously for professional help with the dog's training then a month or two on a refresher course may be invaluable for the youngster's continued improvement and future success.

EXERCISE AND FITNESS

As the summer months run into autumn I begin to prepare my dogs for the shooting season. Again, peak physical fitness is essential if the dog is to put in a full day's strenuous work. For hunting dogs, lessons on bare ground are of little use as any experienced dog will pace itself and not put the required amount of physical effort in to tone the muscles. I find that regular sorties to find rabbit-holding ground are ideal to generate that extra mental stimulation necessary to make the more experienced dog really exert itself sufficiently to turn the summer flab into hard muscle. Swimming can also be an excellent way, especially for retrievers, to regain fitness but some dogs will float lazily if allowed. When using water to aid fitness, I prefer to find a fast-flowing river and practise retrieving against the flow so that the dog really has to use all its strength to reach a dummy on the other bank.

Free Running

Free running exercise can also produce the same results for fitness, but will do untold damage to the dog's discipline; running across open stubble where hares are hiding in shallow forms or diving swallows are in a feeding frenzy can tempt a chase to start, which will undermine previous training. Your close working companion of last season may quickly become a wide-ranging embarrassment if control is not strictly maintained and unnecessary hazards avoided. A fit dog does not have to be lean; the animal must have plenty of hard muscle and energy reserves if stamina is to be sustained throughout the physical excesses endured in the cold winter months.

Grass Seeds

Make sure that, immediately after every outing during the summer months, you check the dog for foreign bodies, particularly in the ears, eyes, coat, or between the toes and pads of the feet. Burrs, thorns and worst of all grass seeds can all cause severe irritations or infections to arise if not dealt with promptly. The most vicious seeds are those from the plant commonly known as barley grass; they are like miniature spears that will pierce the skin and then migrate through the dog's body if left unchecked. These will burrow deep in the ears and feet causing severe pain. The dog will be in obvious distress very quickly, either violently shaking or rubbing its head along the ground, or biting at its feet. The services of your vet should be sought immediately. Smaller, less harmful seeds may just be a temporary inconvenience by getting in the eyes, much the same as us getting a fly in the eye. Careful removal with the corner of a soft tissue and a wash with clean water may be all that is required.

Mental Stimulation

The dog's mental state is just as important as its physical well-being. If you are the person it accompanies when shooting during the winter, you need to keep this bond strong throughout each close season also. Do not hand over the dog's maintenance to someone else; looking after its daily needs may be all that is required to maintain the bond that you have developed. Occasional dummy work and revision of the other aspects of formal training will definitely keep the mutual respect and control alive. Little and often is again the key – be careful not to bore the dog with too much repetition, or worse still in the case of a very enthusiastic 'dummy dog' do not get it so keen to retrieve that steadiness suffers or it begins to make a noise in anticipation of retrieving. Remember how the early retrieving lessons were carried out to maintain steadiness, and still collect at least half of the dummies by hand to keep good discipline.

KENNEL MAINTENANCE

Although some kennel manufacturers may claim that their products are maintenance free, I am afraid that there really is no such thing. Wooden kennels will need regular treatment with wood preserver and, of course, all kennels must be kept clean. You may be lucky and own a very laid-back animal that treats its home with absolute respect, but I can assure you that even this apparently clean home will need regular attention to ensure that germs and bacteria are kept under control.

Most modern kennels are sectional in design and must be erected on a good waterproofed concrete base with adequate slope to ensure that any surface liquid drains away quickly. Concrete that is constantly damp will soon become green, especially in direct sunlight, creating an excellent environment for germs to breed.

Cleaning

After scrubbing with a proprietary cleaning product and then washing down the runs with clean water I always remove any surplus liquid with a wide rubber blade called a squeegee and allow to dry, before spraying with a high quality disinfectant. These are manufactured especially for safe use with dogs to control a range of bacteria, fungi and viruses. Beware of using cheaper products designed for farm or garden use; they can be very harmful to the well-being of your favourite companion if ingested or paddled in.

Bedding

All my dogs are housed in kennels with a wooden sleeping compartment; I try to avoid the use of any loose bedding, which is ideal as a breeding ground for germs and parasites. However, in the severest of weather shredded paper or a piece of Vetbed fleece will keep any dog snug and warm. But two or more dogs cuddled up together maintain a comfortable temperature in the sleeping box, and with all their sensitive extremities tucked out of sight will not come to any harm even in arctic conditions, which are very rare nowadays.

If, however, you are happier to provide your dog with bedding at all times, which of course is more practical if the dog lives in the family home, then I would suggest that you invest in a suitably sized piece of Vetbed. Looking similar to a sheepskin rug, it will allow any dampness to pass through and so like a nappy will stay relatively dry on the surface. It is especially ideal to make a small puppy feel secure, being warm and soft like its mother's fur, and can be easily cleaned in the washing machine. It is fairly expensive, so if your dog is at the chewing stage in its life then I would not recommend using it in kennels but stick to the shredded paper, which is available in compressed bales. Avoid at all costs any form of bedding which if swallowed could cause serious harm, such as synthetic or foam-backed carpet remnants. Bean bags may be excellent for the house dog but I can assure you that they are a nightmare for the kennel owner; being greeted by a happy little black Cocker covered in white polystyrene beads may look cute but when you are still finding them weeks later it is not so funny, and I have no idea what they could do to a dog's digestion.

Parasites

I have already advocated the regular treatment of your dog for skin parasites such as fleas, lice or ticks. It is therefore essential, to avoid re-infestation, that the dog's living quarters are also treated regularly. Although adult fleas spend virtually all their life on the dog they can if unchecked produce vast quantities of eggs which will develop through larval and pupal stages in the kennel environment until the adult stage is reached, when they will re-infest your dog. Regular treatment of the dog's accommodation with a proprietary product will not only kill any insects or parasites immediately but will prevent the unhatched eggs and flea larvae from maturing into adults for several months. The working dog that is also the family pet will possibly, after mixing with other dogs in the course of his master's sport, deposit unwelcome visitors into the family home. It is therefore a sensible precaution therefore to treat the home environment on a regular basis also.

Dogs that have been working will generate a lot of body heat. Barbara Ayres' picking-up team resting in a well-ventilated vehicle between drives at Holme Shoot.

HEAT STROKE

Dogs cannot lose heat by sweating through the skin like humans do, and so they should not be allowed to lie out in the heat of the summer sun. Even though they may have access to water and shade that does not mean they will seek it, particularly when in a heat-induced deep sleep. It would be better if access to the sun was denied by careful management. Similarly, dogs do die in hot cars every summer and many lucky escapees owe their lives to the vigilance of car parking staff at public events. Even in the cooler months, if the sun comes out it can soon turn the interior of a vehicle into an oven with dire consequences. Leaving the top of the windows open will do little to prevent eventual death. Do not think this only applies to dogs left in stationary cars, as there have been several instances where dogs have perished in the back of enclosed vehicles whilst moving.

CONCLUSION

Routine maintenance and personal attention to your dog's needs will ensure a fit, healthy and, most importantly, a happy shooting and family companion for many years to come. This applies equally to dogs that live in the family home or in kennels.

CHAPTER FIFTEEN

Behavioural Problems

Domestic behaviour problems and how to treat them. Shooting field problems and how to treat them, including suggested retraining approaches.

DOMESTIC PROBLEMS

The list of canine behavioural problems that can arise in the family home and also when in other environments is extensive. Likewise, an excellent house dog may have a problem that only arises when out shooting or when housed in a kennel. However, if the dog has been properly reared, socialized and taken through the full training course to make it an obedient companion or a competent working gundog then many of these behaviours will not naturally arise. They can of course still inadvertently be caused or made worse by the family in later life.

Dogs with one problem will usually have faults in other areas of their behaviour. A dog that jumps up, for instance, is not fully under control and this would point to a deficiency in its training. Most domestic problems are induced by the handler or a deficiency in training and subsequent retraining can definitely make improvements, if not effecting a complete cure.

However, those behaviours that are compulsive or caused by phobias are far more complex – fear of thunder, for example. There may also be problems, like sexual mounting or certain types of aggressive behaviour that may need clinical treatment, for which veterinary advice must be sought.

I will restrict my advice to those more common domestic problems that can be rectified through training.

Attention Seeking

Just the same as a child, some dogs constantly seek the attention of their owners. This can happen in different ways but some will keep trying various approaches until a reaction happens, and then of course the behaviour has been reinforced and so is very likely to re-occur. A dog may sit and stare at you, or perhaps keep nudging your arm with its nose; this may be coupled with a whine or a bark. Do not reinforce any of these actions by giving the dog attention; even a look in its direction is all that some dogs need to make them try again.

Play Biting

As soon as puppies in the nest find their feet and begin to play with their siblings so play fighting and biting will begin. This should not be allowed to continue once the puppy has joined the family unit, especially if the family has young members, who are more vulnerable and likely to be pestered by a playful puppy. If toes, fingers and faces are kept away from the puppy's mouth then it will not be able to bite them and so the habit will not develop. Every time a puppy approaches and tries to nibble,

Paige (the author's granddaughter) being pestered by an enthusiastic Ormewood puppy. Who is biting whom?

immediately cease contact and ignore it until such time as it approaches correctly, when reward can be given. Left unchecked or actively encouraged by rough play, biting can develop into a more sinister problem.

Noise

Uncontrolled barking or whining in the adult dog is very often associated with, or a symptom of, one of the other listed problem behaviours, such as attention seeking. It may also be associated with a fear of a strange object or person and could be a warning of impending aggression. The latter is not common in the gundog breeds but that does not mean that it cannot happen. If any noise is rewarded then it will reoccur, but ignoring a dog barking is not always going to be the solution to make it stop; indeed in the majority of cases it will continue. A dog that barks in the garden may be communicating with another canine so far away that it is virtually inaudible to our ears. So the dog must be taught that making an uncontrolled noise is forbidden, through the use of a punisher to stop the noise, when positive reinforcement can then be given to the dog for being quiet. There is also a theory that if you actually teach a dog to bark on command then it follows that it is easier to teach it to be silent on command as well.

Destructive Behaviour

This can be associated with separation anxiety, or just caused by boredom during periods of isolation. If the articles that are being destroyed are small household or personal items then the answer is to remove any such items from the dog's immediate environment. However, if the furniture, door frames or kitchen cupboards are the target then the dog must be removed; perhaps by the use of an indoor kennel for periods when the dog is not under close supervision. To prevent boredom setting in a dog must have plenty of things to stimulate its senses when left alone – a radio playing, a large marrow bone, a canine toy full of treats can all help the time of separation from its owner pass more quickly. Only leave young puppies for very short periods at first, and then if all is well gradually increase the length of time, rewarding all good behaviour.

Climbing on the Furniture

The rules to be followed in the household environment must be clear, consistent and firmly set. They should be adhered to by the dog and by all family members. If during early rearing the puppy was allowed to cuddle up on the sofa, even if it was on your lap, then as it gets older it will believe it is still allowed to use the sofa as a bed. So really the dog does not have the problem, as the rules were not adhered to by the owner.

Looking for a comfy resting place is very different from climbing up over the kitchen table or work surfaces searching for food.

This, of course, is a self-rewarding pastime if food has inadvertently been left out. As a small boy, and so a long time before I began understanding dog training and behaviour modification techniques, I cured our wayward Springer from stealing scraps off the draining board with two strategically placed mousetraps. The first trap, when sprung, had the desired effect and attached itself firmly to her nose! She never climbed up there again.

Jumping Up

During the puppy's early development the family, or visitors to the home, may have inadvertently encouraged the dog to jump up. When a puppy is very small and obviously very cute there is a great temptation to allow it to put its paws on your feet or up your leg as you greet it. All strangers seem to think this is an appropriate way for your little dog to be treated. This relaxation of the rules will over time deteriorate until the puppy is trying to jump up even higher to gain its reward (the person's attention) when it is not immediately forthcoming. This is another symptom of attention seeking. Now the touch of your hands on the pup to push it away is still going to reinforce the action of jumping up and so the behaviour continues to get worse. If the puppy was never rewarded from day one for having two feet off the ground, let alone all four, then this problem would never have started.

To correct it later means training all the humans of the household how to act correctly when meeting the dog so that when the dog comes to them on subsequent occasions behaving boisterously they must now fold their arms, turn their backs and completely ignore it. There must definitely be no eye contact, no touching, no speaking, and no shouting. From now on the dog will only receive a reward when it has all four feet on the ground or, better still, when it is sitting quietly on its bottom.

Thomas and puppy breaking the house rules!

Involuntary Urination when Greeted

Usually this is more likely to occur in puppies and younger adult dogs. The very submissive puppy is more prone to this problem, although sometimes it can be triggered by fear of a stranger; of course if the puppy is reprimanded for doing it then that in itself will make matters worse. As maturity is reached so the problem will diminish or disappear. The way that the dog is approached and greeted can also influence the severity of the problem and whether it is likely to diminish with age. The greeting should always be done calmly, by allowing the dog to come up to you rather than imposing yourself on the dog. Try to avoid causing the dog to be become highly excited and certainly do not tell it off if an accident occurs.

Fear of Strangers

This may be caused by incorrect socialization or a bad experience with a stranger. Gradual desensitization should effect a cure but prevention by correct socialization as a puppy would be far better. Flooding the senses can also work with some pupils, such as taking them on the lead into a public area that is full of people so there is no escape until the dog accepts that it is not going to come to any harm. If there is any sign of aggression being caused by the fear then for the safety of others I would not advocate using the flooding technique.

Scent-Marking the Furniture

Dogs and bitches can both be guilty of this, although it is usually the former that present the biggest problem due to male sexual urges and the height from which the urine is sprayed. It is difficult to stop; close observation and an immediate punishment when the dog is caught in the act is required. In the case of males, castration is another option to reduce those out-of-control testosterone levels, which are causing the dog to mark its territory at every opportunity.

Most family dogs have the freedom to roam the house and this will allow the dog every opportunity to keep re-marking those previously soiled areas. All traces of previous misdemeanours need therefore to be removed using an odour eliminator specifically designed for the purpose. Confinement in an indoor kennel when the owner is otherwise occupied will prevent urination on the furniture but that is not a cure.

The dog must be put through a strict refresher course of basic house-training, and just as if it were a small puppy make sure it uses the designated toilet area in the garden and learns to urinate on a verbal command such as 'Be quick' or 'Hurry up'. This is done by associating the chosen command with the action and then reinforcing the behaviour with a reward. Back indoors complete vigilance is required by the owner; a dog will always give an indication by body language or a slight change in behaviour just before offending. This indication must be recognized so that the dog can be caught in the act of preparing to urinate, before it has actually done it. For the smaller breeds a quick lift, or the larger dogs a lead round the neck is required to take it out to the toilet area in the garden where praise can be given when the dog relieves itself there. It must learn the rules of the house fully and know that this behaviour will not be tolerated.

Sexual Mounting

This applies to mounting people's legs as well as other dogs and if left unchecked during adolescence this can develop into an annoying and more serious habit leading sometimes to aggression. Dog to dog, of course, is fairly natural and even bitches will do this when in season. However, mating a visitor's leg is clearly not acceptable, and neither is this type of behaviour when directed at small children. Young dogs can become highly aroused during rough or energetic play and so sensible management is required to remove any environmental factors that are making this happen. Stop the children having free play with the dog, do not allow the dog to pester visitors but introduce them properly. Separate the offender from other dogs when not under your strict supervision and control. Of course through the use of a correctly timed word of punishment the dog should soon begin to learn that it is not an acceptable pastime. In severe cases medication or castration are possible clinical solutions, which a vet should give advice on.

AGGRESSION

The worst of all domestic problems, aggresson can manifest itself in many different ways for different reasons or causes. Aggression directed toward another dog in certain circumstances can be perfectly natural, but that is different from a real urge to fight all-comers. Aggression towards people is totally inexcusable and must not be allowed to continue. Dogs put in boarding kennels for the first time may be so frightened by the alien environment that, if not approached with caution for the first few days, they may resort to aggression through being in a fearful state.

Confrontational situations must be avoided with any dog that has shown this characteristic. The dog must learn that it is far more rewarding to pay attention to its owner rather than trying to attack other people or dogs. The owner must be the dominant pack member if the dog is going to respond and maintain its lower pack position, which should subdue aggressive tendencies in the home.

Aggression when being Examined or Groomed

Health checks, which may include grooming to remove debris, thorns or dead hair from the coat, must be carried out on a regular basis. If started at a young age the puppy should accept this quite naturally and any attempt to struggle or bite can be stopped quite easily. However, if a dog starts to become aggressive when touched in later life this may be due to a medical condition, such as the onset of arthritis or it may have an injury that is not evident. A thorough clinical examination will identify any medical causes. This is clearly different from a dog with a bad temperament that has decided it is now going to dominate its owner; in these circumstances professional retraining advice may be required.

Travel Sickness

Many young puppies will shows signs of travel sickness when they first get in a car, but the majority grow out of it. Those that continue into adulthood, however, can be helped. It can be caused by fear, excitement, and the motion of the car, fumes from the exhaust or from someone smoking in the vehicle. To cure the problem you first need to identify the cause.

If the dog is afraid of getting in the car in the first place, then when it moves this will only consolidate the fear. Getting a puppy used to the vehicle from an early age will prevent the fear ever starting. Obviously the puppy should not be fed before being put in the car on these early outings. Motion sickness usually does not occur for the first part of the journey, and so short spells in the car up and down the road near the home should gradually get the puppy used to it. Some puppies travel better when they can see out of the window. Many, however, are more settled in the security of a travelling box with solid sides, which stops them watching the horizon going up and down. They will usually shows physical signs before they vomit, such as drooling excessively, becoming restless or dropping their head. Do not reward these signs by offering reassurance by voice or hands. I do not like the use of drugs, as there are side effects such as drowsiness or upset digestion later on.

Picky Eating

Dogs in the wild are certainly not picky eaters; they keep well fed by hunting for prey or by scavenging. They will feed to excess if food is available because they have no way of knowing when they will find food again.

Picky eaters in the home are made this way by the way their food is presented and managed by the owner. Indeed many so-called picky eaters are obese and have lost their appetite. If, however, the dog is fully fit, and a health check by the vet will easily confirm this, there is no reason why it should not then go through a course of remedial training to teach it to eat each meal in one go. For this to be successful in the minimum of time, only one feed a day at a set time will be offered.

Choose a good quality complete diet and stick to it. I personally use a dry food as any that is left can be re-used. Measure out the right quantity for the dog's weight and place it in front of the dog. After ten minutes I remove the bowl, whether it has been touched or not. The dog will now have to wait twenty-four hours until the next scheduled feed time before being offered food again in the same way. There must be no treats, snacks or morsels from the owner's table in the meantime, but ensure free access to water.

Twenty-four hours later the procedure of bowl down, wait ten minutes, then remove is repeated. The survival instinct will eventually take over and the food will be gobbled down. It may take three or four days to achieve the desired result and in extreme cases a little longer but the owner's emotions must not be allowed to interfere. The dog will come to no harm and the result will be a confident eater enabling its food intake to be managed correctly in the future. Once conditioned to eat in this natural way the dog will never again be known as a picky eater.

Eating Stones or Foreign Bodies

There seems no logical reason why a puppy or dog should eat stones. I have experienced only two specimens, one was a Cocker puppy that had been hopper fed on dry food and as soon as it was allowed out in the gravel-covered yard it would gobble down the pebbles, I assume thinking it was food. Luckily they all passed through the digestive system and the puppy came to no harm. She was only eight weeks old when this started; however, once the environment was changed and access to gravelled areas denied until she was over twelve months old, the problem disappeared of its own accord and never re-occurred. The other dog was a Labrador who suffered also from coprophagy and he would gulp the stones down with the faeces that he picked up off gravel. This was different, because the stones were now flavoured with something the dog was actively seeking. Again everything passed through with no ill effects.

Tennis Balls

On the subject of other foreign bodies I do know of a Clumber Spaniel that had seven tennis balls removed from its stomach only just in time to save its life.

If a dog eats any foreign object that is a non-food indigestible item this can cause serious internal problems, and veterinary advice should be sought immediately.

Eating Faeces

A morbid appetite, coprophagy, eating poo are all terms to describe a rather disgusting habit. Unfortunately, to the canine this desire, which causes us disgust and social embarrassment, is a perfectly natural behaviour and does the dog no harm at all, providing of course that worming is carried out on a regular basis. Eating the faeces of other dogs or animals can, however, be a way of contracting other diseases so the dog should be deterred.

There are many reasons for a dog developing this habit. The nursing bitch will eat any waste from the puppies to keep the nest and surrounding area clean and, of course, the puppies may subsequently imitate the mother's behaviour as weaning takes place. To effect a complete cure when the habit has become firmly established in the older dog is not always possible but matters can be improved. To counter-condition the dog that it is more rewarding to move away from the faeces rather than approach to eat it can be accomplished by using a punisher when the dog approaches it and a reward when it moves away from it. Strict vigilance on the owner's part is required if this is to be effective. Keeping the dog's normal toilet area clean and tidy will help and any new faeces should be treated immediately with strong pepper to deter the dog from eating it, and the dog should be rewarded well when it leaves it alone. A muzzle could be used to physically stop any attempt succeeding until you can intervene.

This problem generally seems to be much more prevalent since the introduction of complete foods; dogs reared by the more natural methods of feeding bones and raw flesh do not develop this trait. So it may be worth considering trying a different product to see if that makes an improvement.

Fear of Thunder

You would have thought that after years of selective breeding to produce gundogs that can work regularly with loud bangs in the shooting field this problem would not arise. However, in actual fact the incidence of dogs that are terrified of thunder is quite high; these dogs very often are scared of fireworks also.

Is it strange that they are probably not frightened of gunshot? Fear of the unknown could be the cause. During training the owner will have gone to great lengths to introduce the sound and sight of the gun gradually, probably using systematic desensitization so that gunfire does not induce fear. However, we cannot do the same with thunder and the dog may have been asleep in a dark kennel or alone in the house when this fearful new sound was heard. Imagine how frightening that could have been; with no means of escape as the storm got closer, the dog's fears would have been consolidated. Fear of fireworks can start in the same way; now that they are set off at every possible opportunity it is impossible to make sure that the dog is not isolated the first time it hears them. Very often all the dog requires to help over come this fear is the company of its owner, who can channel its attention away from the fireworks towards something more pleasurable such as food or play. Eventually the sound will be a signal for receiving pleasure and not fear. I cured a working Labrador bitch of mine of her fear of fireworks with a pocket full of food while allowing it to watch an hour-long display at a distance of about 600 metres. By the end of the hour her attention was definitely fully focused on the food.

Self-Mutilation

This is often a symptom of something that requires clinical treatment. A thorn under the skin will irritate the dog and it will continually lick the area to try to alleviate the irritation. This can develop until the hair has all been licked off and the skin is being softened, and eventually the tissue underneath will be exposed. If the dog is really agitated by this increasing soreness it may start to bite at the area and cause serious tissue damage. The same can apply with a dog that has blocked anal glands or is riddled with worms. The anus and surrounding areas can be attacked quite brutally, causing lasting damage if allowed to continue. These causes are easily prevented with regular health checks by the owner, especially after exercise or work, to remove any foreign bodies from the skin or fur. Tail-chasing can deteriorate into the dog actually chewing the end of it.

Boredom is one of the biggest contributing factors of self-mutilation. If the dog is healthy, well looked after, and well stimulated both mentally and physically then this should not occur. If it does then veterinary help must be sought.

Hyperactivity

It really is a difficult job to properly identify whether a working-bred gundog is unusually hyperactive or just that is naturally a very active dog. Spaniels, Cockers in particular, always seem to be on the go, ready for a run or work, which is normal for the breed. I would only consider an individual dog has a problem if it is acting in an abnormally hyperactive way.

Good training will give the dog an 'off switch' which the owner should be able to use when required to put the dog back at rest. The companion dog can become hyperactive prior to its scheduled daily walk and be such a nuisance that although it is blowing a gale and raining persistently the poor owner gives in and takes it out. This of course rewards the hyperactive behaviour and so it re-occurs at the same time every day.

SHOOTING FIELD PROBLEMS

Gun-Shy or Gun-Nervy

It is uncommon for a dog to be completely gun-shy after full training for use with the gun has been carried out. If you have only found out that the dog is slightly gun nervy on its introduction to the shooting field, then something has probably been missed during training. The dog should have been completely desensitized to the sound of the shot and the sight of the weapon before being taken shooting.

However, it is possible that a dog that has been thoroughly trained may still be apprehensive of a loud bang in certain circumstances. I have known dogs ruined through being sat in a pigeon hide or duck blind; whilst the owner was blazing away in front, the dog was quivering behind unnoticed until too late. Even the worst cases can and should be improved for the sake of the dog having a happy life. Systematic desensitization definitely works and I have cured several bad cases using this method.

Hard Mouth

The cause of a hard mouth with the young dog in training can simply be tension or over-excitement when confronted with a new, very appetizing object. A quantity of retrieves in quick succession, as could be provided on a driven pheasant shoot, may possibly be all that is required to relax the dog's grip to overcome this. However, with others it is much more complex and the trainer's actions when the dog delivers can have a huge bearing on the cause and the outcome.

Ill-Timed Anger

It would be only too easy to show disappointment or anger at the time when the dog is damaging the game or when it delivers it to hand. The anger would of course make the situation worse by developing mistrust, tension or fear in the dog as it approaches you on subsequent occasions. Whatever the damage you must never tell the dog off for returning to you with a retrieve. In fact a dog should not be told off when it returns to you under any circumstances. I just grin and bear it at the time when it occurs, then pause to analyse the events which may have caused it before deciding what subsequent actions are required or what retraining is possibly going to effect a cure.

If the habit has only begun when the dog is getting older then a remedial programme of training will not work. The dog has probably learned through experience, perhaps being spurred by a pheasant or kicked by a rabbit, that lifeless game is easier to retrieve and is not likely to cause it pain.

Giving Tongue, Whining or Barking

Once a gundog has developed the annoying habit of making a noise in its work it is virtually impossible to eradicate. Whining on the drop is usually indicative of incomplete basic training, when the dog should have been taught to remain calm when motionless. Perhaps the introduction to the shooting field has been rushed, the over-excitement causing the noise to develop. Many dogs are completely mute whilst in motion, yet the inactivity of sitting and waiting at the peg or in a hide can cause this high-pitched whine to begin in anticipation of the enjoyment of searching for game to retrieve.

The problem can even worsen to the point where opening the gun cabinet at home is the sign for the dog to start, and by the time the owner has suffered the dog's noise or hyperactivity all the way to the shoot he surely cannot still be friends with his canine companion. The whine that a dog first tentatively emits is usually of such a high pitch that only the ears of the youngest trainers can detect it; by the time it is audible to the rest of us the problem could already be an irreversible habit.

Early Training

A puppy that has been completely mismanaged in the first eighteen months of life and has received little if any correct basic training is more likely to bark and whine than if it had undergone a sensible course of training. Even a small puppy must be guided along the right track; I have seen people teaching their new charge to bark for food or as a signal to be let out into the garden during house training. This may be desirable for the family pet, but they are laying the seeds for noise problems later on if the dog is going to be used for work, i.e. barking when their owner is preparing to go shooting. Puppies in play have plenty of free time to enjoy each other's company without human intervention, and barking, quite naturally, is a part of this. However, they must be taught that making a noise in other circumstances, such as in their quarters at rest, will not be tolerated or rewarded.

Barking for Attention

I try to avoid situations that create a set routine that influences the young dog's behaviour pattern. If you feed a puppy at exactly the same time over a period of weeks, then one day you forget, the hungry youngster will become agitated to the point of making a noise to attract attention. This reminds you of your mistake and you immediately present the dog with a bowl of food to quieten it down. You are in fact rewarding the dog for its last behaviour, barking.

Deterrents

Perhaps this may seem a little unjust considering the mistake was of the trainer's own creation, but instead of a bowl of food a squeeze of the jowls and a verbal scolding would in the long run be more beneficial. However, I find that stopping the noise by averting the dog's attention, for example by tossing stones on the kennel roof, is less likely to upset the bond I am trying to build with the puppy than by using my presence or voice. Only once the dog has remained quiet for a suitable period should the bowl of food then be given, which also gives a reward for its quietness.

The Impact of Breeding

The dog whose only crime is to yip when being sent out to retrieve may not be a problem to the rough-shooter. However, it is an indication perhaps of a failure in its genetic make-up, which could pass on to future generations if the dog is bred from. It is for this reason that great care needs to be taken from the start. Choose a puppy from a good working/field trial strain; noisy animals are eliminated from competition and should therefore be omitted from the parent stock of successful breeders.

Running In

Most young dogs are steady to shot and flush when they are first introduced to the shooting field. As they gain experience of direct contact with game then their enthusiasm to work also increases, and if you are not careful a keen dog will begin to pre-empt or anticipate being sent to retrieve. Avoidance is better than trying to cure the problem once it is well established. Sensible management and control are needed to maintain the level of training that the dog has already achieved. The dog at the peg will begin to anticipate working immediately after the drive has finished if that is what it is has continually been allowed to do. If every time a spaniel flushes a rabbit, it is subsequently allowed to retrieve it straight away then that is what it will begin to anticipate doing immediately it flushes one. The slightest movement, after a flush or as a bird is falling, should be corrected and the dog must not be rewarded with the retrieve. If the handler maintains their own self-discipline then their dog is more likely to do the same. A thorough refresher of the steadiness training using dummies is advisable.

Chasing Fur

This can suddenly develop but usually there are indications that a breakdown in steadiness is going to occur. The hunting dog is more prone to develop this than the retriever that is walking or sitting at heel. The cause can be similar to running in, only these dogs are moving long before the gun has got involved. Unfortunately if the game they are chasing is shot then they are instantly rewarded with the retrieve. On no account should shooting expeditions be continued, but instead a refresher course in the rabbit pen is the first essential programme of retraining to carry out. The dog must recognize the sight or smell of a moving rabbit as a cue to stop hunting immediately.

Chasing Birds

Few dogs that have been properly trained are prone to chase birds later on, perhaps because any that try are, except in exceptional circumstance, unable to catch one and so the natural

Sally using the walking stick to encourage Purdey to keep level.

defeat lessens the urge to behave this way again. You will usually find that a dog that is chasing birds has other concerns regarding its steadiness, and remedial training using the rabbit pen should be carried out.

Not Delivering but Dropping Game

A poor delivery, if not corrected during training, will only get worse until the dog eventually refuses to deliver the retrieve at all, or perhaps releases wounded game before it is safely in the owner's grasp. When fully trained, the dog should ideally lift its head up towards the handler on its return, so that the retrieve can easily be removed gently from its mouth with one hand (I am assuming that the gun is being carried in the other). I am afraid that in practice this ideal delivery is not achieved by every aspiring trainer. I have recently spent some considerable time on a well-bred English Springer Spaniel dog which continually refused to bring a retrieve of any description right in to hand; instead he would throw the dummy on the floor and lay both his front feet on top of it. Every time I put my hands anywhere near him, his tongue would dart swiftly over my hands. I used various methods to try to induce him to hang on to his prize, but eventually I decided to gently 'force' the delivery as described in an earlier chapter. This produced a complete cure, which resulted in a proper delivery.

However, if a dog suddenly begins to drop game in the shooting field when it previously had no problem at all during training then you need to identify why this has suddenly occurred. Injury or infection in the dog's mouth could be the cause and the solution then would not be retraining.

Delivery from Water

It is quite common for a dog to stop and shake as it leaves water with a retrieve; it really should not put the game down to do this.

Wounded duck, for instance, will soon scrabble back in and then dive under the water to escape all subsequent attempts at re-capture. It is no good rushing up to the dog shouting 'Hold' as this will probably make matters worse. Standing well back from the bank may encourage a speedier and complete return.

Shaking on Command
The other theory that can be applied in practice with patient and lengthy training is to teach the dog only to shake on command; then the situation can be fully controlled. This training should not be combined with retrieving but done in isolation until it has been perfected. The dog is recalled across a stream or small river whilst the trainer stands right by the water's edge so that the dog can be stopped as soon as it leaves the water and told to sit. It must be rewarded well for sitting, then after a pause, give the clear verbal command, 'Shake'. As the training progresses so the distance the handler stands from the water can be increased until the dog has been firmly conditioned only to get up from the sit and then to shake on command.

Heelwork
It is fairly common for dogs to begin walking in front of their handlers, rather than by their side, once the dog has learned the enjoyment of working on live game. It is only being really keen to watch what is going on, to mark game that is shot, or perhaps pre-empting being allowed to hunt. However well-schooled it was during formal training this can be a real problem and for the sake of safety when you are carrying a gun it should not be allowed. This is the one time where the walking stick is used during training, to swing across in front of its nose so it maintains the correct position at your side.

CONCLUSION

With correct training and management a dog should live a relatively problem free life in social harmony. Many of the above domestic and shooting field problems are a symptom of another underlying cause, or they are the result of incorrect management or training. It is much easier to prevent problems ever arising than it is to effect a complete cure.

Epilogue

Whilst the title of this book may have suggested that it was just about training the dog you should now, after reading it, be aware that it is actually more about teaching you, the person, who will be your dog's trainer.

Without human influence in a dog's life, no matter how well-bred a puppy is, it will never achieve the necessary social and working skills that are required in the modern family or in the shooting field. It may instead revert to some of those primeval instincts that were possessed by its distant ancestors in the wolf pack.

You as the trainer will fulfil the role of pack leader and earn the respect of your dog through the positive learning experience that I have previously described.

Patience is important and the most impatient person, if they are committed to this task, will find the self-discipline to develop the necessary patience. If you can only concentrate fully for ten minutes then that is sufficient. Likewise, the canine mind has a short attention span so do not extend lessons just to suit your ability – the dog has feelings to!

There are several important points to try to remember:

- Never give an order to the dog that you cannot enforce compliance with. It is no good blowing the stop whistle if the dog is coursing a rabbit on the far side of a river; you will only confirm that the dog is being disobedient.
- Never lose your temper. When things go wrong, put the dog away and calm down, have a cup of tea and think about what occurred before attempting the exercise again.
- Never think you know it all. When I first began gundog training Jimmy Wylie said to me, 'When you have been doing this for twenty years, only then will you begin to learn.' I thought he was joking, but I know now that he was not, as after thirty years new knowledge still keeps flooding in. Seek advice or discuss concerns with your peers.
- Never give a command and subsequently punish the dog. Your dog is chasing a rabbit, you shout 'Sit', the dog sits and then you wade in and tell it off. Do you think it will be inclined to sit next time?
- Always give praise when the dog is doing something right. Associate a reward with a desired behaviour and that behaviour is more likely to re-occur.
- Do not reward a dog that is doing something wrong. If you do not reward a particular behaviour then that behaviour is less likely to re-occur.
- Likewise if you associate a punisher with a behaviour, then that behaviour is less likely to re-occur (a punisher can just be the withdrawal of a reward).
- Always end each lesson on a good note. If things go wrong then do something you know the dog will definitely succeed at, rewarding it amply so that you part as friends

CONCLUSION

I thoroughly enjoy my country pursuits and the dogs that are an integral part of the family and shooting scene. My methods have stood the test of time and so I hope this book will encourage and inspire many more to take part in this fascinating, rewarding pastime and enjoy their dogs to the full.

An enjoyable pastime, one for the future.

Further Information

ORGANIZATIONS

THE KENNEL CLUB
1–5 Clarges Street,
Piccadilly,
London W1J 8AB

Telephone: 0870 606 6750
Website: www.thekennelclub.org.uk includes direct links and contact numbers for all Kennel Club services, including the Working Gundog Certificate and KCAI.

BRITISH VETERINARY ASSOCIATION
7 Mansfield Street,
London W1G 9NQ

Telephone: 020 7636 6541
Website: www.bva.co.uk/public/chs (for information on health screening).

THE BRITISH ASSOCIATION FOR SHOOTING AND CONSERVATION
Marford Mill,
Rossett,
Wrexham LL12 0HL

Telephone: 01244 573000
Website: www.basc.org.uk

COUNTRYSIDE ALLIANCE
The Old Town Hall,
367 Kennington Road
London SE11 4PT

Telephone: 020 7840 9200
Website: www.countryside-alliance.org

NATIONAL GAMEKEEPERS' ORGANISATION
PO Box 107,
Bishop Auckland DL14 9YW

Telephone: 01388 665899
Website: www.nationalgamekeepers.org.uk

THE SPANIEL CLUB
Website: www.thespanielclub.co.uk

MAGAZINES

SHOOTING TIMES
Telephone: 020 7261 6180
Website: www.shootingtimes.co.uk

DOG WORLD
Telephone: 01233 621877
Website: www.dogworld.co.uk

INTERNET SITES

SPORTING GUNDOGS.COM
A website with links to other sites of interest in the UK and Ireland.

Telephone: 0845 006 8865
Website: www.sportinggundogs.com

DOG FOOD AND EQUIPMENT SUPPLIERS

CHUDLEYS DOG FOOD
Telephone: 01832 737300
Website: www.chudleys.co.uk

MASTERS DOG FOOD
Telephone: 01327 811758
Website: www.mastersdogfoods.co.uk

SKINNERS DOG FOOD
Telephone: 01379 384247
Website: www.skinnerspetfoods.co.uk

LINTRAN TRANSIT BOXES
Dog travelling boxes and trailers
Telephone: 01673 885959
Website: www.lintran-products.co.uk

QUEST GUNDOG TRAINING EQUIPMENT
Telephone: 01257 425222
Website: www.questgundogs.co.uk

THE DUMMY SHOT
Telephone: 0777 155 3004
Website: www.thedummyshot.co.uk

PAUL FRENCH VIDEO
Telephone: 01778 341255
Website: www.gundogvideos.com

CROMESSOL Air De-odorizing Disinfectant
Telephone: 01698 354 600
Website: www.cromessol.co.uk

ORMEWOOD KENNELS

ORMEWOOD BOARDING KENNELS & CATTERY

Email: lynrawlings@btinternet.com

Index